Super Food in Minutes

This book is dedicated to our brilliant online community of home cooks, who cook these recipes with such enthusiasm and passion – thank you for sharing your dinners with me!

Super Food in Minutes

Donal Skehan

HODDER &
STOUGHTON

First published in Great Britain in 2019
by Hodder & Stoughton
An Hachette UK company

Copyright © Donal Skehan 2019
Photography by Issy Croker © Hodder & Stoughton 2019

A CIP catalogue record for this title is available from the British Library.

Hardback ISBN 978 1 529 32558 4
eBook ISBN 978 1 529 32559 1

Senior Commissioning Editor: Tamsin English
Project Editor: Natalie Bradley
Copy-editor: Clare Sayer
Nutritionist: Kerry Torrens
Designer: Nathan Burton
Photographer: Issy Croker
Food and Prop Stylist: Emily Ezekiel
Senior Production Controller: Susan Spratt

Colour origination by Altaimage
Printed and bound in Germany by Mohn Media

Hodder & Stoughton policy is to use papers that are natural, renewable and recyclable products
and made from wood grown in sustainable forests. The logging and manufacturing processes
are expected to conform to the environmental regulations of the country of origin.

Hodder & Stoughton Ltd
Carmelite House
50 Victoria Embankment
London EC4Y 0DZ

www.hodder.co.uk
www.donalskehan.com

Follow Donal at @donalskehan on Twitter and Instagram
and at /donalskehan on Facebook and YouTube.

Contents

Introduction

Our morning routine almost always starts at 6am, almost always with porridge. Noah, our one-year-old, is wide-awake and babbling to himself. These are those precious moments before he turns into an incoherent dictator and begins to make breakfast demands from his cot. To get ahead of this I slink into the kitchen followed by our dog Max, who knows this routine all to well – the calm before the storm. Once the porridge pot is on the stove, my wife Sofie has strapped Chairman Noah to the high chair and it's go time, we're in play, it's full-on family mode! And it doesn't stop until we all reconvene for dinner in the evening, when after a busy day dinner needs to be quick and nutritious.

Juggling family and work life is non-stop – something I'm sure many people can relate to – and in order to cook and eat well, planning and preparation are key. After writing eight cookbooks, I find myself, now more than ever, fine-tuning my recipes to make them genuinely easy, requiring only a stripped-down ingredients list and ensuring that they can be made in minutes. There was a time when I would come home and spend a couple of hours pottering away in the kitchen, and perhaps that time will return, but as our family grows, quick dinner fixes are key. There are plenty of recipes out there that can be whipped up in a matter of minutes, but for this book I wanted to bring that idea to the next level to provide you with a playbook of recipes that not only produce speedy suppers, but also just so happen to be good for you too!

Like most food lovers, I find it hard to shy away from a perfectly cooked steak doused in nutty brown butter or the smell of roast chicken on a Sunday but now more than ever, I am drawn to recipes that are vibrant and veggie-forward, not just from a health point of view but from an environmental one too. With so much information going back and forth on vegan, vegetarian and the many other diets we are bombarded with, it can be confusing to make the right choices, but I firmly believe that at the core of good nutritious food are high-quality meats, good fats, whole grains and as many vegetables as you can fit on your plate!

While my last book *Meals in Minutes* provided a collection of hearty, comforting family meals, *Super Food in Minutes* puts an emphasis on practical, nourishing, veg-forward family food that brings healthy ingredients to the fore. I want to give you the building blocks of functional cooking and recipes that really work for busy lifestyles, proving that you can make really spectacular meals at the drop of a hat. This is 'healthy food' for food lovers! Dig in!

Happy Cooking!

Donal x

What is *Super Food in Minutes?*

Super Food in Minutes is all about real, fast and delicious family food that just so happens to be good for you! With these 90 recipes I will help you change the way you cook using recipes, tips and hacks for home cooks that are looking for speedy meals as well as balance in their diets.

Quick cooking, as any busy home cook will know, is an essential skill. The growing interest in veg-forward eating that is not only good for you but is also good for the planet, means that health-conscious cooks are increasingly looking for uncomplicated ways to bring food to the table. *Super Food in Minutes* is a celebration of recipes and ideas that will provide busy families with real food fast, food that packs a nutritional punch and delivers big on flavour. Taking inspiration from the diets and eating habits of the world's blue zone areas – those places in the world where people live longer and healthier lives than anywhere else – means that there is a much greater emphasis on vegetables, whole grains, good fats and smaller amounts of high-welfare, organic meats.

The promise

With just ten ingredients or fewer and requiring completely pared-back kitchen basics and a cooking time of 30 minutes or less, each recipe uses streamlined, quick-cooking methods with minimal effort and maximum results that will help you make the most of your time spent in the kitchen. Each recipe includes a nutritional breakdown and cook's notes, and is laid out in a way that is clear and easy to follow. Exceptional everyday good-for-you meals made with healthy ingredients should be achievable for everyone and are at the core of this book, helping you bring dinner to the table in half the time!

A guide to the recipe layout

Nutritional labels

You will find nutritional labels underneath the recipe title, so you can easily see how many portions of fruit and vegetables are in one serving, as well as spot if a recipe is vegetarian or vegan.

 PORTIONS OF FRUIT AND VEGETABLES

 VEGETARIAN

 VEGAN

Equipment

I've included key equipment in this section, but make sure you have to hand the usual suspects that aren't listed here, like a chef's knife and a wooden spoon.

Ingredients

Every recipe features 10 ingredients or fewer, not including core ingredients:

Olive oils (regular and extra-virgin)

Neutral cooking oil (I use sunflower oil)

Sugar

Salt and freshly ground black pepper

Measurements

Imperial measurements or cups are listed next to the metric. See the conversion chart on page 221 for more information.

Nutritional information

The nutritional information at the bottom of each recipe was provided by a qualified nutritionist. The figures are for one serving and exclude serving suggestions or optional items and garnishes.

All the Greens Pasta

(2)

Serves:	Equipment:	Cook's Notes:
4	Deep sauté pan with lid	About as simple as it gets – toss it all in the pan, give it a little stir, then just stand back and wait for supper to appear.

350g (12oz) linguine or spaghetti

240g (8½oz) tenderstem broccoli, trimmed

2 tbsp extra-virgin olive oil

500ml (2 cups) fresh chicken or vegetable stock

bunch of asparagus (about 250g/9oz), trimmed

150g (5oz) frozen peas

4 spring onions, thinly sliced

75ml (⅓ cup) single cream

20g (¾oz) Parmesan cheese, grated

finely grated zest of 1 lemon

handful of basil leaves

1. Take a large, deep sauté pan and lie the linguine in the middle. Arrange the broccoli around the linguine. Drizzle with the oil, pour in the stock and season well with salt and pepper.

2. Cover and bring to the boil, then reduce the heat and simmer for 8 minutes, stirring every so often to stop the pasta sticking. Add the asparagus, peas and spring onions, and cook for 3–4 minutes more.

3. Add the cream, Parmesan and lemon zest, and cook for 1–2 minutes more until you have a lovely saucy, creamy pasta. Serve with a scattering of basil leaves and a grinding of black pepper.

COOK'S TIP

Make it veggie: swap the Parmesan for a vegetarian alternative and make sure you use vegetable stock.

KCALS	FAT	SAT FAT	CARBS	SUGARS	FIBRE	PROTEIN	SALT
510	13.0g	4.0g	73.0g	7.0g	10.0g	20.0g	0.45g

A note on shopping for ingredients

One of my first jobs was doing work experience with my aunt Erica, who works as a food stylist. I was 13 and mesmerised by the fact that she got to play with food for a living. One of the first times I helped her she taught me how to shop properly for ingredients. Writing out a list with the sections of the shop in mind made life a whole lot easier when it came to filling three shopping trolleys with ingredients. It's a simple trick that saves you darting back and forth across the supermarket floor and it's one I still use if I'm doing a big shop for a meal plan. I've laid it out like this in each meal plan to give you a headstart.

Another element of my shopping routine starts as soon as I get in the door with bags of ingredients. I aim to put away most things, but anything that I can get ready to the next stage I do at that moment. Fill a salad spinner with water and clean your veggies and salad leaves, whisk up salad dressings, put on a tray of veggies to roast, peel carrots and store them in cold water, shave cabbage and other hardy veg for quick salads – basically any small job that will help you cut down on waste and ultimately form the building blocks of some great meals.

The meal-planning mindset

I'd love to tell you that our family meals evolve on a whim from a nice jaunt to the farmers' market, but in all honesty, they rely on organisation, planning and preparation. It might not sound too exciting, but those three key elements are what prevent baby meltdowns and general parent 'hanger' towards one another. We learned quickly on the journey to parenthood that keeping everyone well fed was in all our interests!

One of the key aspects of making our kitchen work is meal planning. As I typically work from home, at the start of this new habit I was overambitiously planning breakfasts, lunches, dinners and snacks, all different every day, resulting in interminable shopping lists that weren't sustainable and leftovers bulging out of the fridge. Now, real meal planning for us comes down to the simple process of laying out just five key dinners across the week. Only choosing five key meals allows for flexibility around the inevitable chopping and changing life throws your way, and means that you will always be armed with the ingredients to bring dinner to the table in minutes.

To bring a little spontaneity to proceedings, I leave the weekends open to allow for eating out or maybe cooking something I've been wanting to try or a meal that takes a little more time. I also leave space on the shopping list for things that might grab my attention while out shopping. I've learned that flexibility is key, but having that core plan of five meals provides a focus. Here I've laid out four weekly meal plans from the recipes in this book, which should give you some meal planning inspiration and show you how you make the process simple. I hope these meal plans kick-start a new approach and strategy to dynamic food that works for your schedule.

Week 1 meal plan

MONDAY	TUESDAY	WEDNESDAY	THURSDAY	FRIDAY
Harissa Chicken with Rainbow Salad	Kale Cacio e Pepe	Charred Pork Banh Mi Salad	One-pan Tomato & Bean Fish Chowder	Spiced Kebab Platter

Shopping list for 4 people

VEGETABLES & FRUIT	MEAT, POULTRY & FISH	STORECUPBOARD	FRIDGE
2 onions (1 red, 1 white)	6 boneless, skinless chicken thighs	1 x 400g (14oz) tin chickpeas	Unsalted butter
Bunch of spring onions	500g (1lb 2oz) pork tenderloin	1 x 400g (14oz) tin cannellini beans	Pecorino cheese
Garlic	4 x 150g (5oz) haddock fillets	600ml (2½ cups) passata	Hummus
2 lemons	500g (1lb 2oz) lamb mince	500ml (2 cups) vegetable stock	Low-fat Greek yoghurt
1 avocado		400g (14oz) dried spaghetti	
300g (10oz) kale		Rose harissa paste	
1 x 220g (8oz) bag rainbow salad		Fish sauce	
1 romaine lettuce		Rice wine vinegar	
3–4 carrots		Pine nuts	
1 red chilli		Ras el hanout	
½ cucumber		4 flatbreads	
500g (1lb 2oz) soffritto mix or vegetable soup mix			
Flat-leaf parsley			
Coriander			
Basil			

Week 2 meal plan

MONDAY	TUESDAY	WEDNESDAY	THURSDAY	FRIDAY
Krapow Chicken	Brown Butter Brussels Sprouts Salad with Crunchy Grains	All the Greens Pasta	Crispy Salmon with Asparagus & Cherry Tomato Sauce	Spring Lamb

Shopping list for 4 people

VEGETABLES & FRUIT	MEAT, POULTRY & FISH	STORECUPBOARD	FRIDGE & FREEZER
2 small onions	8 boneless, skinless chicken thighs	200g (7oz) cooked quinoa	Unsalted butter
Garlic	4 skin-on salmon fillets	75g (2½oz) walnuts	Single cream
2 Thai red chillies	8 lamb leg steaks	350g (12oz) linguine or spaghetti	Parmesan cheese
300g (10oz) Brussels sprouts		1 litre (4 cups) fresh chicken or vegetable stock	Frozen peas
Bunch of spring onions		White wine vinegar	
240g (8½oz) tenderstem broccoli		Dijon mustard	
500g (1lb 2oz) asparagus		Reduced salt soy sauce	
150g (5oz) cherry tomatoes		Fish sauce	
1 dessert apple		Oyster sauce	
2 lemons			
250g (9oz) new potatoes			
3 baby gem lettuces			
50g (2oz) mixed micro herbs			
Thai basil			
Basil			
Flat-leaf parsley			

Week 3 meal plan

MONDAY	TUESDAY	WEDNESDAY	THURSDAY	FRIDAY
Aubergine Curry with Turmeric Cauliflower Rice	Scallops with Green Peas & Asparagus	Lemon, Chilli & Garlic Pan-fried Mackerel with Quick Butter Bean Stew	'Roast' Chicken Dinner	General Tso's Tofu Stir-fry

Shopping list for 4 people

VEGETABLES & FRUIT	MEAT, POULTRY & FISH	STORECUPBOARD	FRIDGE & FREEZER
2 onions	12 fat king scallops	1 x 400g (14oz) tin chopped tomatoes	Natural yoghurt
Garlic	4 whole mackerel	2 x 400g (14oz) tins butter beans	Frozen peas
Fresh ginger	8 skin-on chicken thighs	Ground turmeric	Unsalted butter
3 aubergines		Nigella seeds or black mustard seeds	Parmesan cheese
800g (1lb 12oz) riced cauliflower		Garam masala	250g (9oz) block extra-firm tofu
1 bunch of asparagus		150ml (2/3 cup) vegetable stock	
160g (5½oz) kale		250ml (1 cup) chicken stock	
300g (10oz) baby spinach		Dijon mustard	
300g (10oz) baby new potatoes		Cornflour	
200g (7oz) baby carrots		Rice vinegar	
1 red chilli		Reduced salt soy sauce	
2 lemons		Hoisin sauce	
Rosemary		Soft brown sugar	
Mint		Sesame oil	
Thyme			
Flat-leaf parsley			

Week 4 meal plan

MONDAY	TUESDAY	WEDNESDAY	THURSDAY	FRIDAY
One-pan Chicken Parmesan	Brassica Caesar Salad	Thai Green Curry Noodle Soup	Miso Sesame Green Beans with Crusted Tuna	Chickpea & Greens Tagine

Shopping list for 4 people

VEGETABLES & FRUIT

350g (12oz) courgette spaghetti

320g (11¼oz) broccoli florets

150g (5oz) kale

150g (5oz) Brussels sprouts

2 aubergines

300g (10oz) tenderstem broccoli

170g (6oz) sugar snap peas

2 spring onions

2 red onions

1 large fennel bulb

2 medium courgettes

1 red pepper

250g (9oz) vine tomatoes

200g (7oz) spring greens

320g (11¼oz) green beans

1 red chilli

1 lemon

1 lime

Garlic

Fresh ginger

Basil

Coriander

Flat-leaf parsley

MEAT, POULTRY & FISH

500g (1lb 2oz) mini chicken breast fillets

4 x 120g (4oz) tuna steaks

STORECUPBOARD

300ml (1¼ cups) passata

1 x 400ml (14fl oz) tin reduced-fat coconut milk

400ml (1¾ cups) vegetable stock

100g (3½oz) vermicelli rice noodles

1 x 400g (14oz) tin chickpeas

Panko breadcrumbs

Sourdough bread

Pine nuts

Green curry paste

Capers

Nutritional yeast

Red miso paste

Reduced salt soy sauce

Rice vinegar

Dried oregano

Dried thyme

Ras el hanout

FRIDGE

Hummus

Mozzarella cheese

Parmesan cheese

A note on getting ahead, and leftovers

Around the time we were getting ready for our son Noah's arrival I began to get into the habit of cooking more than just breakfast in the morning. It started as a way to get ahead for those delirious few weeks at the start of parenthood. If I had time, I'd fry off chicken in spiced butter, make veggie chilli or blitz together quick soups, all to be bunged into the freezer or fridge for dinner and for the sleep-deprived days ahead. Those little moments in the morning, where cooking dinner didn't feel like a chore, allowed me to get ahead and at least create the bones of, if not the whole meal. So many of our meals were saved from ordering a takeout because we had the core of a supper, ready to rock. Even after those wobbly first months had passed, this little routine has endured and helps so much when it comes to our family meals. In fact, as much as I talk about cooking quick meals, we often find ourselves sitting down to dinner comprised of leftovers or made up from these pre-prepped ingredients. Harissa chicken thighs cooked that morning, a tangy cabbage salad spiked with toasted fennel seeds from a lunchbox in the fridge with a dollop of tahini garlic yoghurt: these are all key elements that are ready to go once dinnertime rolls around.

For our family, lunch often works in the same way; rather than one single dish, we're more inclined to build a plate with a mezze of leftovers, spruced up with fresh herbs, a squeeze of lemon juice and a drizzle of good olive oil, or sprinkled with toasted seeds and spices – this way even the saddest-looking leftovers can be transformed. It's also a great way to keep track of what's hanging out in your fridge after a week of meals.

Many of the elements of the recipes in this book lend themselves extremely well to being made ahead and also to being used in other dishes. Dressings, sauces and cooking methods can be interchanged with different salads, meats and vegetables. I encourage you to experiment as you go.

One-pan Suppers

There are plenty of impressive dinners you can whip up using just one pan, and this chapter is filled with them! There's ease to the one-pan method, but the true success comes at the end of the meal where the clean-up is minimal. These suppers are diverse in flavour, but what ultimately unifies them is that they all have simplified cooking methods.

Korean Kimchi Tomato Eggs

(3) (V)

Serves:
2

Equipment:
Frying pan
with lid

Cook's Notes:
A wonderful fusion of Middle Eastern shakshuka
with the flavours of Korean bibimbap.

1 tbsp sesame oil

75g (2½oz) beansprouts

1 carrot, peeled and julienned

1 tbsp sesame seeds, toasted

2 tsp sunflower oil

1 red onion, thinly sliced

2 garlic cloves, crushed

1 x 400g (14oz) tin chopped
tomatoes

200g (7oz) kimchi

4 large free-range eggs

handful of coriander leaves

1. Heat the sesame oil in a frying pan and gently fry the beansprouts and carrot until just softened and fully heated through. Tip into a bowl with the sesame seeds.

2. Heat the sunflower oil in the same frying pan and gently fry the onion for 5 minutes until softened, then add the garlic and fry for 1 minute. Add the chopped tomatoes and kimchi, season with salt and pepper and cook for 10 minutes.

3. Make four hollows in the sauce using the back of a spoon and crack the eggs into them. Cook for 8–10 minutes until they are just set (cover to speed up the cooking). Serve with the carrot and beansprouts and a scattering of coriander leaves.

KCALS	FAT	SAT FAT	CARBS	SUGARS	FIBRE	PROTEIN	SALT
287	16.0g	3.0g	19.0g	15.0g	6.0g	12.0g	0.88g

Black Bean Tofu Stir-fry

(2) (VG)

Serves:	**Equipment:**	**Cook's Notes:**
4	Large frying pan	Making your own black bean sauce, while easy to do, is quite time-consuming, so save precious minutes by using a top-quality shop-bought one instead.

200g (7oz) vermicelli rice noodles

1 tbsp sunflower oil

280g (9¾oz) firm tofu, drained and sliced into finger-width pieces

2 small red chillies, deseeded

3 garlic cloves, crushed

2cm (¾in) piece of ginger, peeled and grated

6 tbsp black bean sauce

bunch of spring onions, thinly sliced

2 red peppers, deseeded and sliced

250g (9oz) sugar snap peas

1. Soak the noodles in boiling water for 10 minutes, then drain.

2. Heat half the oil in a large frying pan over a medium–high heat. Pat the tofu with kitchen paper so it is nice and dry and then fry in the pan for a few minutes on each side until golden. Transfer to a plate lined with kitchen paper and set aside.

3. Return the pan to a medium–high heat, add the chillies, garlic and ginger and fry for 2 minutes until fragrant, then add the black bean sauce and 100ml (½ cup) water. Tip into a bowl and wipe the pan clean with kitchen paper.

4. Add the rest of the oil to the pan and fry most of the spring onions and the red pepper over a high heat for 3–4 minutes, or until just tender. Add the black bean sauce from the bowl and the sugar snap peas and fry for 3–4 minutes until the paste is aromatic and the sugar snap peas are tender.

5. Add the drained rice noodles and tofu, toss to coat and heat through thoroughly. Serve garnished with the reserved spring onions.

KCALS	FAT	SAT FAT	CARBS	SUGARS	FIBRE	PROTEIN	SALT
409	10.0g	1.0g	54.0g	9.0g	8.0g	21.0g	1.50g

General Tso's Tofu Stir-fry

Serves:
4

Equipment:
Wok or deep frying pan

Cook's Notes:
General Tso refers to the sauce rather than the dish itself – this sweet sticky sauce, usually served with chicken, is a staple of North American Chinese restaurants.

250g (9oz) block extra-firm tofu

2–3 tbsp cornflour

4 tbsp sunflower oil

For the sauce

3 tbsp rice vinegar

3 tbsp reduced salt soy sauce

1 tbsp hoisin sauce

1 tbsp soft brown sugar

1 tbsp sesame oil

2cm (¾in) piece of ginger, peeled and grated

2 garlic cloves, thinly sliced

1 red chilli, very thinly sliced

1. Cut the tofu into 2cm (¾in) cubes and dry well on kitchen paper. Put half the cornflour into a food bag, add the tofu cubes and toss to coat, then add the remaining cornflour and toss again. Set aside for 5 minutes to become slightly tacky.

2. Mix the rice vinegar, soy sauce, hoisin sauce and brown sugar together in a bowl and set aside.

3. Heat the sunflower oil in a wok or frying pan over a high heat and cook the tofu for 1–2 minutes on each side until golden brown. Remove from the pan and set aside to drain on kitchen paper. Drain any excess oil from the wok.

4. Allow the wok to cool a little, then add the sesame oil, ginger, garlic and chilli and gently fry for about 1 minute before adding the blended sauce ingredients with 150ml (²/₃ cup) water. Bubble until you have a thick, glossy sauce.

5. Return the tofu to the pan and toss to coat all over. Serve with steamed basmati or brown rice and broccoli.

KCALS	FAT	SAT FAT	CARBS	SUGARS	FIBRE	PROTEIN	SALT
304	19.0g	3.0g	20.0g	7.0g	2.0g	11.0g	1.21g

One-pan Vegetable Lasagne

(2)

Serves:
6

Equipment:
Ovenproof
sauté pan

Cook's Notes:
This is a fab veggie version of that comfort food favourite lasagne – just without all the pots and pans to wash up!

2 tbsp olive oil

2 small onions, finely chopped

3 garlic cloves, crushed

3 courgettes, chopped

250g (9oz) cremini or button mushrooms, sliced

1 x 400g (14oz) tin chopped tomatoes

200g (7oz) baby spinach

400g (14oz) fresh pasta sheets, sliced into strips

handful of fresh basil leaves, torn

80g (3oz) Parmesan cheese, grated

2 x 125g (4oz) mozzarella balls, sliced

1. Heat the oil in a deep, ovenproof sauté pan. Add the onions and fry over a medium heat for 5 minutes until softened, then add the garlic and cook for a minute more.

2. Add the courgettes and mushrooms, increase the heat and fry for about 5 minutes until they are lightly browned. Add the chopped tomatoes and 400ml (1¾ cups) boiling water and season well with salt and pepper. Bring to a simmer and cook for 10 minutes over a medium heat.

3. Preheat the grill to high. Stir the spinach and pasta strips into the pan and, once the spinach has wilted, stir in the basil and two-thirds of the Parmesan and half the mozzarella. Scatter the rest of the cheese over the top and put under the grill for 3–5 minutes until bubbling and oozingly melty.

COOK'S TIP

Make it veggie:
swap the Parmesan
for a vegetarian
alternative.

KCALS	FAT	SAT FAT	CARBS	SUGARS	FIBRE	PROTEIN	SALT
449	19.0g	9.0g	43.0g	7.0g	5.0g	24.0g	0.73g

All the Greens Pasta

Serves:	Equipment:	Cook's Notes:
4	Deep sauté pan with lid	About as simple as it gets – toss it all in the pan, give it a little stir, then just stand back and wait for supper to appear.

350g (12oz) linguine or spaghetti

240g (8½oz) tenderstem broccoli, trimmed

2 tbsp extra-virgin olive oil

500ml (2 cups) fresh chicken or vegetable stock

bunch of asparagus (about 250g/9oz), trimmed

150g (5oz) frozen peas

4 spring onions, thinly sliced

75ml (⅓ cup) single cream

20g (¾oz) Parmesan cheese, grated

finely grated zest of 1 lemon

handful of basil leaves

1. Take a large, deep sauté pan and lie the linguine in the middle. Arrange the broccoli around the linguine. Drizzle with the oil, pour in the stock and season well with salt and pepper.

2. Cover and bring to the boil, then reduce the heat and simmer for 8 minutes, stirring every so often to stop the pasta sticking. Add the asparagus, peas and spring onions and cook for 3–4 minutes more.

3. Add the cream, Parmesan and lemon zest and cook for 1–2 minutes more until you have a lovely saucy, creamy pasta. Serve with a scattering of basil leaves and a grinding of black pepper.

COOK'S TIP

Make it veggie: swap the Parmesan for a vegetarian alternative and make sure you use vegetable stock.

KCALS	FAT	SAT FAT	CARBS	SUGARS	FIBRE	PROTEIN	SALT
510	13.0g	4.0g	73.0g	7.0g	10.0g	20.0g	0.45g

Lemon, Chilli & Garlic Pan-fried Mackerel

with Quick Butter Bean Stew

Serves:
4

Equipment:
Large frying pan

Cook's Notes:
The butter bean stew would also go brilliantly with other fish such as pan-fried sea bream or salmon fillets.

2 tbsp olive oil

4 whole mackerel, filleted

20g (¾oz) knob unsalted butter

1 onion, finely chopped

2 garlic cloves, crushed

2 sprigs of rosemary

2 x 400g (14oz) tins butter beans, drained and rinsed

300g (10oz) baby spinach

finely grated zest of 1 lemon, plus a squeeze of juice

150ml (⅔ cup) vegetable stock

handful of flat-leaf parsley, chopped

1. Heat half the oil in a large frying pan over a low–medium heat. Season the fish fillets with salt and pepper and score the skin a couple of times. Add to the pan, skin-side down, and gently fry for 3–4 minutes until golden and crisp. Carefully turn the fish over, add the butter and cook for 1 minute until just cooked through. Transfer to a plate and keep warm while you make the stew.

2. Heat the remaining oil in the same pan and gently fry the onion for 5–10 minutes until really softened and golden. Add the garlic and rosemary and cook for 1 minute, then tip in the butter beans, spinach and lemon zest. Add the stock and cook for 1 minute to wilt the spinach. Season well.

3. Add the parsley and a squeeze of lemon juice to the beans, then spoon into shallow bowls. Top with the crispy mackerel fillets.

KCALS	FAT	SAT FAT	CARBS	SUGARS	FIBRE	PROTEIN	SALT
853	60.0g	15.0g	19.0g	4.0g	10.0g	54.0g	1.07g

Miso Sesame Green Beans

with Crusted Tuna

Serves:
4

Equipment:
Frying pan
with lid

Cook's Notes:
It's worth splashing out on good tuna steaks for this
Japanese-inspired supper, which would be the perfect
dish for entertaining friends.

2 tbsp sunflower oil

3 tbsp red miso paste

2cm (¾in) piece of ginger,
peeled and grated

2 tbsp reduced salt soy sauce

1 tbsp rice vinegar

320g (11¼oz) green beans

1 tbsp white sesame seeds

1 tbsp black sesame seeds

4 x 120g (4oz) tuna steaks

1. Heat half the oil in a frying pan and gently fry the miso
   paste and ginger for 1 minute before increasing the heat
   and adding the soy sauce, rice vinegar and green beans,
   along with a splash of water. Cover and cook the beans
   for 4–5 minutes until tender and glazed. Transfer the
   beans to four plates and, using kitchen paper, wipe the
   frying pan clean.

2. Meanwhile, mix the white and black sesame seeds
   together and use most of them to coat the tuna steaks.
   Heat the remaining oil in the frying pan over as high
   a heat as possible. Sear the tuna steaks for 45 seconds
   to 1 minute on each side; you want them browned but
   still very rare in the middle.

3. Serve the miso beans with the tuna steaks and the
   remaining sesame seeds scattered over. Brown rice
   makes a good accompaniment.

KCALS	FAT	SAT FAT	CARBS	SUGARS	FIBRE	PROTEIN	SALT
257	10.0g	2.0g	6.0g	4.0g	4.0g	34.0g	2.41g

Tomato & Summer Vegetable Braised Chicken

Serves:	**Equipment:**	**Cook's Notes:**
4	Large sauté pan with lid	Step into summer with this veggie-packed, light chicken casserole.

1 tbsp olive oil

4 chicken breasts, butterflied

1 red onion, cut into thin wedges

2 garlic cloves, bashed

4–5 sprigs of thyme

3 small courgettes, cut into batons

200g (7oz) new potatoes, thinly sliced

400g (14oz) chopped vine tomatoes

250ml (1 cup) fresh chicken stock

320g (7¼oz) green beans

finely grated zest of 1 lemon, plus a squeeze of juice

1. Heat a tiny drizzle of the oil in a large sauté pan. Season the chicken all over with salt and pepper and brown really well over a high heat until golden – this should take about 2–3 minutes. Remove from the pan and set aside.

2. Add the rest of the oil to the pan, reduce the heat to medium and gently fry the onion, garlic, thyme and courgettes for 8 minutes until the onion is just softened and the courgette has started to brown.

3. Add the potatoes, tomatoes and stock, then return the chicken to the pan and simmer, partially covered, for 10 minutes until the potatoes are tender and the chicken is cooked through.

4. Add the green beans and lemon zest and cook for 2 minutes more until the beans are just tender. Stir in a squeeze of lemon juice and serve.

KCALS	FAT	SAT FAT	CARBS	SUGARS	FIBRE	PROTEIN	SALT
377	10.0g	1.0g	16.0g	9.0g	7.0g	51.0g	0.60g

Honey Garlic Chicken

Serves:
4

Equipment:
Large sauté pan
with lid

Cook's Notes:
The classic combo of sticky garlicky chicken with an
Asian twist.

1 tbsp olive oil

8 chicken thighs

6 garlic cloves, thinly sliced

3 tbsp clear honey

3 tbsp white wine vinegar

3 tbsp reduced salt soy sauce

200g (7oz) broccoli,
broken into florets

250g (9oz) sugar snap peas

bunch of spring onions,
sliced into 2cm (¾in) pieces

handful of coriander leaves

1 tbsp sesame seeds

1. Heat the oil in a large sauté pan, season the chicken with
   salt and pepper and add to the pan skin-side down. Fry for
   6–8 minutes until really golden.

2. Flip the chicken over and add the garlic, honey, vinegar
   and soy sauce and bubble for 5 minutes.

3. Add the broccoli, sugar snaps and spring onions and cook,
   stirring to combine, for 6–8 minutes more until the chicken
   is cooked through. Serve sprinkled with coriander leaves
   and sesame seeds.

KCALS	FAT	SAT FAT	CARBS	SUGARS	FIBRE	PROTEIN	SALT
340	19.0g	5.0g	18.0g	15.0g	4.0g	21.0g	1.23g

Krapow Chicken

Serves:
4

Equipment:
Frying pan

Cook's Notes:
Also called Thai basil chicken, this is one of the most delicious Thai dishes going. Thai basil is pretty widely available now, not only from Asian shops but online and in many big supermarkets. I like to serve mine with some tenderstem broccoli for an extra hit of green.

2 tbsp sunflower oil

2 small onions, thinly sliced

2 garlic cloves, crushed

2 Thai red chillies, finely chopped

8 boneless, skinless chicken thighs

2 tbsp reduced salt soy sauce

1 tbsp fish sauce

1 tbsp oyster sauce

large bunch of Thai basil

1. Heat the oil in a frying pan and gently fry the onions for 5 minutes until softened. Add the garlic and chilli and cook for 1–2 minutes more.

2. Use a sharp knife to slice the chicken as finely as possible. Add the chicken to the pan and increase the heat to brown the chicken all over.

3. Add the soy, fish and oyster sauces and cook until the chicken is cooked through and glazed in the sauce. Meanwhile, heat the rice according to the packet instructions.

4. Remove the pan from the heat and stir through the Thai basil. Serve with jasmine rice and steamed tenderstem broccoli.

KCALS	FAT	SAT FAT	CARBS	SUGARS	FIBRE	PROTEIN	SALT
294	16.0g	3.0g	8.0g	2.0g	1.0g	28.0g	2.07g

'Roast' Chicken Dinner

Serves:
4

Equipment:
Deep sauté pan
with lid

Cook's Notes:
All the flavour of a full Sunday roast, but in a speedy
one-pan supper.

1 tsp olive oil

8 skin-on chicken thighs

finely grated zest of 1 lemon,
plus a squeeze of juice

3 sprigs of thyme,
leaves picked

300g (10oz) baby new
potatoes, halved

200g (7oz) baby carrots,
halved lengthways

250ml (1 cup) chicken stock

2 tsp Dijon mustard

160g (5½oz) kale, tough stems
removed and leaves shredded

handful of flat-leaf parsley,
roughly chopped

1. Heat the oil in a large deep sauté pan over a medium heat.

2. Season the chicken thighs generously with salt and pepper
   and place skin-side down in the pan with the lemon zest,
   thyme and potatoes.

3. Allow the chicken thighs and potatoes to cook without
   moving for 10–15 minutes, or until the chicken skin turns
   crisp and a deep golden brown colour. Turn the chicken
   and potatoes, add the carrots and cook for 2–3 minutes
   until the carrots are starting to become tender.

4. Combine the chicken stock and mustard, then add to the
   pan. Bring to a simmer, then add the kale. Season, cover
   and cook for 10 minutes more until the chicken is cooked
   all the way through, the potatoes and carrots are tender
   and the liquid has reduced slightly.

5. Serve straight to the table with a good squeeze of lemon
   juice and a generous sprinkling of parsley.

KCALS	FAT	SAT FAT	CARBS	SUGARS	FIBRE	PROTEIN	SALT
316	16.0g	4.0g	13.0g	3.0g	5.0g	28.0g	0.93g

Thai-style Meatballs

Serves:
4

Equipment:
Mini food processor, frying pan

Cook's Notes:
If you don't have a food processor you can bash the paste ingredients in a pestle and mortar instead; it will be a bit chunkier but have all the same flavour. Serve the meatballs as they are or with cooked rice.

500g (1lb 2oz) pork mince

1 red chilli, deseeded and finely chopped

2 garlic cloves, crushed

4 spring onions, thinly sliced

large handful of coriander, stalks and leaves separated

1 tbsp sunflower oil

1 x 400ml (14fl oz) tin reduced fat coconut milk

200g (7oz) tenderstem broccoli, trimmed

250g (9oz) sugar snap peas

1 tbsp reduced salt soy sauce

2 tsp fish sauce

1. Season the mince with some salt and pepper and shape into 12–16 meatballs.

2. Put the chilli, garlic, green parts of the spring onions, coriander stalks and a splash of water into the bowl of a mini food processor and blitz until you have a smooth paste.

3. Heat a little of the oil in a frying pan over a high heat, and fry the meatballs until brown all over. Remove from the pan and set aside, then add the rest of the oil and fry the green paste for 2–3 minutes until aromatic. Add the coconut milk and bring to a simmer.

4. Return the meatballs to the pan and add the broccoli and sugar snap peas. Season with the soy and fish sauces and cook for 3–4 minutes until the vegetables are tender and the meatballs are cooked through. Serve scattered with coriander leaves and the white parts of the spring onions.

KCALS	FAT	SAT FAT	CARBS	SUGARS	FIBRE	PROTEIN	SALT
462	23.0g	11.0g	7.0g	4.0g	3.0g	29.0g	1.24g

Pork Drunken Noodles

Serves:
4

Equipment:
Wok or large
frying pan

Cook's Notes:
Supposedly so-called because they are the perfect match
for a chilled beer, or indeed for a hangover. However, even
without the sore head, these aromatic spicy noodles will
really hit the spot.

250g (9oz) thick flat
rice noodles

1 tbsp sunflower oil

6 garlic cloves

2 bird's-eye chillies,
finely chopped

1 x 175g (6oz) packet baby
corn, halved lengthways

3 pak choi, quartered

250g (9oz) pork loin fillet,
thinly sliced

2 tbsp oyster sauce

1 tbsp fish sauce

1 tbsp reduced salt soy sauce

2 tsp caster sugar

handful of Thai basil leaves

1. Soak the noodles in boiling water for 10 minutes until
   softened. Drain and set aside.

2. Heat half the oil in a wok or frying pan and fry the garlic
   and chillies over a medium–high heat for 1 minute, then
   add the baby corn and pak choi and fry for 3–4 minutes
   more until just tender. Scoop out and set aside.

3. Add the rest of the oil to the pan and fry the pork over a
   high heat until golden. Return the baby corn and pak choi
   to the pan with the drained noodles, add the oyster, fish
   and soy sauces and sugar and stir-fry vigorously to combine.
   Fry until the sauce coats everything and thickens slightly.
   Serve with a scattering of Thai basil.

KCALS	FAT	SAT FAT	CARBS	SUGARS	FIBRE	PROTEIN	SALT
308	13.0g	3.0g	28.0g	5.0g	3.0g	18.0g	2.47g

Spiced Kebab Platter

Serves:
4

Equipment:
Frying pan
with lid

Cook's Notes:
This quick and tasty supper is a million miles from the standard kebab-shop fare. If you have fresh herbs to hand, coriander or parsley adds a fresh bite.

1 red onion, thinly sliced

juice of 1 lemon

2 tbsp olive oil

1 onion, finely chopped

2 garlic cloves, crushed

75g (2½oz) pine nuts, toasted

1 tbsp ras el hanout,
plus extra to serve

500g (1lb 2oz) lamb mince

4 flatbreads

4 heaped tbsp hummus

4 tbsp low-fat Greek yoghurt

1. Put the sliced red onion in a bowl with some salt and pepper, add the lemon juice and set aside to pickle lightly for about 10 minutes.

2. Meanwhile, heat the oil in a frying pan, add the chopped onion and gently fry for 5 minutes until softened. Add the garlic and all but a scattering of the pine nuts and cook for 1 minute more. Add the ras el hanout and cook for 1 minute, then add the lamb mince and season well. Cook over a medium–high heat for about 10 minutes, breaking it up with a wooden spoon, until it is browned all over. Then add a splash of water and cover and cook for 1–2 minutes more.

3. Warm the flatbreads and spread each with a generous dollop of hummus. Scatter over the cooked lamb mince and then top with the pickled red onion, remaining pine nuts and the yoghurt. Finish with a sprinkle of ras el hanout and serve.

KCALS	FAT	SAT FAT	CARBS	SUGARS	FIBRE	PROTEIN	SALT
781	45.0g	10.0g	51.0g	10.0g	7.0g	39.0g	0.77g

Spring Lamb Supper

with Baby Gem, New Potatoes & Peas

Serves:	Equipment:	Cook's Notes:
4	Large frying pan with lid	As winter comes to a close, celebrate the new season with this dish that is packed with all the flavours of spring.

1 tbsp olive oil

8 lamb leg steaks

250g (9oz) new potatoes, halved

350–400ml (1½–1¾ cups) fresh chicken stock

20g (¾oz) unsalted butter

3 baby gem lettuces, quartered

150g (5oz) frozen peas

2 tsp white wine vinegar

2 tsp Dijon mustard

handful of flat-leaf parsley, finely chopped

1. Heat the oil in a large frying pan over a medium–high heat. Season the lamb with salt and pepper and brown all over until just cooked, then remove to a plate and set aside.

2. Add the potatoes to the pan and pour in the stock so it just covers the potatoes; season with salt and pepper. Cover and cook for 10 minutes.

3. Remove the lid and add the butter, baby gem and peas. Fry in the buttery juices for 2–3 minutes, then add the vinegar and mustard. Return the lamb to the pan and cook for 1–2 minutes more to warm through. Serve sprinkled with the parsley.

KCALS	FAT	SAT FAT	CARBS	SUGARS	FIBRE	PROTEIN	SALT
528	32.0g	14.0g	14.0g	5.0g	6.0g	43.0g	1.07g

Mongolian Beef

Serves:
4

Equipment:
Wok or deep
frying pan

Cook's Notes:
Another classic favourite from the Chinese takeaway,
but it's so much better when you make it yourself.

500g (1lb 2oz) sirloin steak,
thinly sliced

1 tbsp cornflour

3 tbsp sunflower oil

3 garlic cloves, crushed

2.5cm (1in) piece of ginger,
peeled and grated

4 spring onions, cut into
2cm (¾in) lengths

300g (10oz) bag stir-fry
vegetables

½ tsp chilli flakes

1 tbsp reduced salt soy sauce

2 tbsp soft brown sugar

275g (9½oz) pack fresh
egg noodles

1. Toss the steak strips in the cornflour and some salt and
   pepper and set aside for 5 minutes. Heat half the oil in a
   wok or frying pan over a high heat and fry the steak until
   browned all over. Remove and set aside.

2. Heat the rest of the oil and fry the garlic, ginger and spring
   onions over a medium heat for 2 minutes. Add the stir-fry
   vegetables to the pan with a splash of water and fry for
   1 minute before adding the chilli flakes, soy sauce and
   sugar along with 200ml (¾ cup) water. Return the steak
   to the pan with the noodles and bubble until you have a
   glossy sauce that coats the noodles. Serve straight away.

KCALS	FAT	SAT FAT	CARBS	SUGARS	FIBRE	PROTEIN	SALT
481	24.0g	7.0g	35.0g	13.0g	3.0g	29.0g	0.85g

Steak & Grilled Greens Fajita Night

2

Serves:	Equipment:	Cook's Notes:
4	Large griddle pan	Put a sizzle in your supper with this all-in-one fajita recipe.

2 tbsp olive oil

1 green pepper, deseeded and sliced

2 baby gem lettuces, cut into wedges

bunch of spring onions, trimmed

350g (12oz) sirloin or rib eye steak

1 tsp ground cumin

1 tsp hot smoked paprika

4 flour tortillas

1 avocado, sliced

150ml (⅔ cup) soured cream

lime wedges, to serve

1. Heat half the oil in large griddle pan, add the green pepper and baby gem wedges and sear all over. Remove from the pan and set aside, then griddle the spring onions until charred all over. Remove from the pan and slice in half.

2. Toss the steak in a bowl with the cumin and paprika, some salt and pepper and the rest of the oil. Add to the griddle pan and sear for 2–3 minutes on each side for medium rare. Remove the steak from the pan and allow to rest before slicing thinly.

3. While the steak rests, return the greens to the pan and toss to coat in the pan juices and warm through.

4. Serve the veggies and steak pieces in flour tortillas with the avocado and dollops of soured cream and lime wedges to squeeze over.

KCALS	FAT	SAT FAT	CARBS	SUGARS	FIBRE	PROTEIN	SALT
500	32.0g	12.0g	26.0g	5.0g	6.0g	24.0g	0.82g

Supper Salads

The days of miserable iceberg lettuce salads are well behind us; in their place are vibrant, colourful and multi-textured plates that celebrate both flavour and seasonal vegetables. When I turn to lighter eating, the recipes in this chapter are a perfect representation of what I like my plate to be filled with: good grains, rainbow-coloured vegetables and intriguing flavour combinations.

Minty Pea & Bean Platter

Serves:
4

Equipment:
Large saucepan, small frying pan

Cook's Notes:
Even in the middle of winter you can make this great summery vibe salad – just use frozen peas and broad beans and leave out the sugar snaps for the taste of high summer in a bowl any time of year.

200g (7oz) raw peas

200g (7oz) raw broad beans

150g (5oz) sugar snap peas

75g (2½ oz) wild rocket

zest and juice of 1 lemon

3–4 tbsp extra-virgin olive oil

handful of baby mint leaves

2 tbsp olive oil

100g (2 cups) fresh white breadcrumbs

1 fat garlic clove, crushed

2 x 125g (4oz) buffalo mozzarella balls

25g (1oz) pecorino shavings

1. Bring a large saucepan of water to the boil. Blanch the peas, beans and sugar snaps for 2 minutes, then drain and cool under running water. If you have time, gently squeeze the broad beans out of their skins to reveal their bright green insides. Add all the beans and peas to a bowl with the rocket.

2. Mix the lemon juice with plenty of seasoning, then gradually whisk in the extra-virgin olive oil and mint leaves. Pour over the beans, peas and rocket.

3. Heat the olive oil in a small frying pan and gently fry the breadcrumbs with the lemon zest and garlic until golden. Drain on kitchen paper and season lightly.

4. Divide the greens between four plates, top each with half a torn ball of mozzarella and a scattering of the crispy crumbs and pecorino shavings, and serve straight away.

COOK'S TIP

Make it veggie: swap the pecorino for a vegetarian alternative.

KCALS	FAT	SAT FAT	CARBS	SUGARS	FIBRE	PROTEIN	SALT
458	30.0g	12.0g	20.0g	3.0g	8.0g	23.0g	1.21g

Jewelled Herb & Rice Salad

(2) (V)

Serves:
4

Equipment:
Sauté pan
with lid

Cook's Notes:
If you have a little extra time, soak the rice in cold water
for 30 minutes before you start cooking. This kick-starts
the water absorption process so that when you cook
the rice you end up with fluffy separate grains that are
perfectly cooked and don't stick together.

250g (9oz) basmati rice

2 tbsp olive oil

30g (1oz) unsalted butter

2 small onions, finely chopped

1 tsp ras el hanout

4 carrots, peeled and grated

pinch of saffron threads,
soaked in 3 tbsp hot water

200g (7oz) mixed dried fruit
such as sultanas, dried
barberries or cranberries

75g (2½oz) shelled pistachios,
roughly chopped

handful of chopped
mint leaves

handful of chopped
flat-leaf parsley

1. If you have soaked the rice, drain and give it a final rinse;
   if not, rinse well in a colander under the cold tap.

2. Heat the oil and butter in a sauté pan, add the onions and
   ras el hanout and fry over a medium heat for 5 minutes
   until softened. Add the drained rice, carrots and saffron
   (with its soaking water), then cover with 300ml (1¼ cups)
   cold water.

3. Season with salt and pepper, stir and bring to the boil. Cover,
   reduce the heat and simmer gently for 12–15 minutes. Turn
   off the heat and leave to stand with the lid on for 5 minutes.

4. Fluff up the rice with a fork, stir in the dried fruit, pistachios
   and herbs, and serve.

KCALS	FAT	SAT FAT	CARBS	SUGARS	FIBRE	PROTEIN	SALT
412	15.0g	4.0g	59.0g	28.0g	6.0g	7.0g	0.16g

Shaved Cauliflower Salad

with Herbs & Spiced Butter Drizzle

Serves:
4

Equipment:
Saucepan

Cook's Notes:
If you want to make this an even more substantial supper, serve with some crumbled feta cheese or slices of fried halloumi.

1 large cauliflower

1 x 400g (14oz) tin chickpeas, drained and rinsed

1 tsp cumin seeds, toasted

150g (5oz) green beans

25g (1oz) flaked almonds, toasted

large handful of chopped flat-leaf parsley

small handful of chopped coriander

juice of ½ lemon

drizzle of extra-virgin olive oil

20g (¾ oz) unsalted butter

2 tsp rose harissa paste

1. Using a sharp knife thinly shave the cauliflower and transfer to a large bowl. Add the chickpeas and cumin seeds and stir together.

2. Blanch the beans in a saucepan of boiling water for 2–3 minutes until just tender but still with some crunch. Drain and cool under cold running water. Add to the cauliflower.

3. Add the almonds, herbs, lemon juice and a drizzle of oil and mix everything together.

4. Melt the butter and harissa paste together with salt and pepper (use the same saucepan you used to cook the beans in). Drizzle over the salad, toss well and serve.

KCALS	FAT	SAT FAT	CARBS	SUGARS	FIBRE	PROTEIN	SALT
256	12.0g	3.0g	20.0g	7.0g	9.0g	12.0g	0.15g

Brown Butter Brussels Sprout Salad *with Crunchy Quinoa*

Serves:
4

Equipment:
High-sided frying pan, small saucepan, fine-meshed sieve, mandolin, sharp knife or food processor

Cook's Notes:
You need to cook the quinoa in plenty of hot oil to get that crunch, but don't be alarmed by deep-frying – it's actually healthier than shallow-frying as food absorbs less oil when deep-fried in hot oil than when slow-fried in a smaller amount of cooler oil. Just make sure you drain well on kitchen paper.

200g (7oz) cooked quinoa

150ml (⅔ cup) olive or sunflower oil, for frying

300g (10oz) Brussels sprouts

1 dessert apple, cored

20g (¾oz) unsalted butter

75g (2½oz) walnuts

4 spring onions, thinly sliced

50g (2oz) mixed micro herbs

25g (1oz) Parmesan shavings

For the dressing

1 tbsp white wine vinegar

2 tsp Dijon mustard

3 tbsp extra-virgin olive oil

COOK'S TIP

Make it veggie: swap the Parmesan for a vegetarian alternative.

---

1. Spread the cooked quinoa out on some kitchen paper and leave to dry for 10 minutes.

2. Pour the oil into a high-sided frying pan and deep-fry the quinoa for 2 minutes until golden and crisp. Remove with a fine-meshed sieve, drain on kitchen paper and season lightly.

3. Shave the sprouts on a mandolin (or shred them using a sharp knife or a food processor) and put into a bowl. Thinly slice and then julienne the apple and add to the sprouts.

4. Melt the butter in a small saucepan over a medium heat until browned and nutty. Pour over the sprouts and apple and toss well.

5. Toast the walnuts in a dry frying pan, roughly chop and add to the bowl with the spring onions and micro herbs. Toss through the crispy quinoa.

6. To make the dressing, mix the vinegar with the mustard and some seasoning, then whisk in the oil. Pour over the sprouts, toss well and scatter with the Parmesan shavings.

KCALS	FAT	SAT FAT	CARBS	SUGARS	FIBRE	PROTEIN	SALT
470	39.0g	8.0g	16.0g	5.0g	6.0g	11.0g	0.47g

Griddled Radicchio Plate

with Spiced Tahini Yoghurt & Blitzed Sesame

 (V)

Serves:
4

Equipment:
Griddle pan,
small frying pan,
pestle and mortar

Cook's Notes:
There are some fabulous varieties of radicchio available these days, so look out for pretty pink, red-flecked white ones and baby ones, as well as the more usual red radicchio. Their bitter flavour is the perfect match for salty, tangy feta and creamy yoghurt.

800g (1lb 12oz) radicchio
(about 4 small heads)

olive oil, to drizzle

150g (5oz) feta cheese,
crumbled

large handful of coriander,
leaves picked

large handful of flat-leaf
parsley, leaves picked

2 tbsp tahini

150g (5oz) low-fat
natural yoghurt

1 large garlic clove, crushed

½ tsp cumin seeds, toasted

good squeeze of lemon juice

2 tbsp sesame seeds

1. Cut the radicchio into wedges, keeping the root intact so it holds together, and drizzle with a little oil to gently coat. Place a griddle pan over a high heat and cook the radicchio in batches for about 1 minute on each side to blacken slightly.

2. Transfer to a serving plate and add the crumbled feta and herb leaves.

3. Mix the tahini, yoghurt, garlic, cumin and lemon juice together and season well.

4. Toast sesame seeds in a dry frying pan until lightly golden, then crush in a pestle and mortar. Drizzle the dressing over the salad, scatter with the crushed sesame seeds and serve.

COOK'S TIP

Keep it veggie:
check the packaging
on the feta to make
sure it is vegetarian.

KCALS	FAT	SAT FAT	CARBS	SUGARS	FIBRE	PROTEIN	SALT
251	17.0g	7.0g	7.0g	7.0g	6.0g	14.0g	1.22g

Brassica Caesar Salad

 (2) (VG)

Serves:
4

Equipment:
Roasting tin,
small frying pan

Cook's Notes:
Nutritional yeast is a staple of a lot of vegan recipes as it gives a salty umami kick to dishes that would usually rely on flavour-packed ingredients such as Parmesan or anchovies. It is easily found in health food shops, but you can swap for vegan Parmesan or regular Parmesan if you prefer.

320g (11¼oz) broccoli florets

4 tbsp olive oil

150g (5oz) kale, tough stems removed and leaves shredded

150g (5oz) Brussels sprouts, finely shredded

100g (3½ oz) sourdough bread, cubed

75g (2½oz) pine nuts, toasted

For the dressing

4 tbsp hummus

2 garlic cloves, crushed

juice of 1 lemon

2 tsp capers, drained and rinsed

2 tbsp nutritional yeast
(see Cook's Notes)

1. Preheat the oven to 200°C (180°C fan).

2. Toss the broccoli in 1 tablespoon of the oil, season well and tip into a small roasting tin. Roast for 15 minutes until lightly golden and tender.

3. Meanwhile, put the kale into a salad bowl with another tablespoon of the oil and massage with your fingers to soften it. Add the shredded sprouts and roasted broccoli.

4. Heat the remaining oil in a small frying pan and fry the sourdough cubes over a medium heat until golden. Add to the bowl with the toasted pine nuts.

5. To make the dressing, mix the hummus, garlic, lemon juice, capers and nutritional yeast together until blended and dollop over the salad before serving.

KCALS	FAT	SAT FAT	CARBS	SUGARS	FIBRE	PROTEIN	SALT
498	34.0g	3.0g	25.0g	5.0g	10.0g	18.0g	1.20g

Sweet Potato & Cauliflower *with Turmeric Yoghurt*

(3) (V)

Serves:
2

Equipment:
Microwave, saucepan with frying pan

Cook's Notes:
This delicious nourishing bowl is packed with flavour and goodness.

2 medium sweet potatoes (about 400g/14oz), peeled and cut into 2cm (¾in) dice

3 tbsp olive oil

1 red onion, thinly sliced

1 medium cauliflower, broken into florets

2 tsp black mustard seeds

1–2 green chillies

1 tsp garam masala

squeeze of lemon juice

½ tsp ground turmeric

200g (7oz) low-fat natural yoghurt

handful of coriander leaves, chopped

1. Put the cubed sweet potato in a microwaveable bowl with 1 tablespoon of water. Cover tightly with cling film and microwave for 10 minutes.

2. Meanwhile, heat 2 tablespoons of the oil in a saucepan and gently fry the onion for 6–8 minutes. Add the cauliflower, mustard seeds, chillies and garam masala. Season and fry for 2 minutes, then add a splash of water, cover and allow the cauliflower to steam for 5 minutes until tender.

3. Heat the remaining tablespoon of oil in a frying pan over a medium–high heat. Add the sweet potato and fry for about 5 minutes until the edges are golden.

4. Stir the sweet potato into the cauliflower, then divide between four bowls and add a little squeeze of lemon juice to each. Mix the turmeric with the yoghurt and dollop on to the bowls. Scatter with coriander leaves and serve.

KCALS	FAT	SAT FAT	CARBS	SUGARS	FIBRE	PROTEIN	SALT
494	20.0g	3.0g	56.0g	32.0g	12.0g	16.0g	0.36g

Scandi Salmon & Cracked Potato Salad

Serves:	**Equipment:**	**Cook's Notes:**
4	Sauté pan with lid	Some things are just meant to be put together, and rich oily salmon with creamy dill and piquant pickle is one such perfect match. If you wanted to mix things up you could try this with hot-smoked mackerel instead.

500g (1lb 2oz) new potatoes

20g (¾oz) unsalted butter

small bunch of dill, finely chopped

1 small red onion, thinly sliced

juice of ½ lemon

½ cucumber

8–10 radishes

200g (7oz) hot smoked salmon

For the dressing

1 tbsp creamy horseradish

2 tbsp half-fat crème fraîche

good squeeze of lemon juice

1–2 tbsp extra-virgin olive oil

1. Put the potatoes in a single layer into a sauté pan with a lid (don't use a non-stick one or you won't get the lovely colour on the potatoes) and just cover with water. Add the butter and some seasoning, cover and bring to the boil. Cook for 5 minutes, then remove the lid and continue to cook until the potatoes are tender and the water has almost evaporated.

2. Lightly crush the potatoes with a fork, so that they just crack open, then add most of the dill (save some for the dressing). Continue to cook over a high heat for 5–6 minutes until the potatoes are golden underneath. Turn the potatoes over and cook for 5–6 minutes more. Season well.

3. Meanwhile, put the onion into a bowl with some seasoning and the lemon juice and set side to lightly pickle. Shave the cucumber into long ribbons. Add to the pickled onion and set aside. Thinly slice the radishes and flake the salmon.

4. To make the dressing, whisk together the horseradish with the crème fraîche, lemon juice and oil. Add plenty of seasoning and the reserved dill.

5. Allow the potatoes to cool a little, then toss with the pickled onion and cucumber, the radishes and flaked salmon. Drizzle with the dressing, toss together and serve.

KCALS	FAT	SAT FAT	CARBS	SUGARS	FIBRE	PROTEIN	SALT
318	18.0g	6.0g	21.0g	5.0g	3.0g	16.0g	1.21g

Niçoise Salad

①

Serves:
4

Equipment:
2 saucepans

Cook's Notes:
Olives cured with the stone inside have so much more favour that the often rather sad pitted black olives. A good tip to make stoning them easy is to push lightly on each olive with your thumb; you will feel the stone loosen inside the olive, you can then tear it open and remove the stone.

400g (14oz) new potatoes

4 large free-range eggs

125g (4½oz) green beans

150g (5oz) sun-blushed tomatoes

1 x 160g (5½oz) tin sustainable tuna in olive oil, drained

50g (2oz) black olives, stoned

1 tbsp capers, drained and rinsed

For the dressing

1½ tbsp red wine vinegar

1 tsp Dijon mustard

3 tbsp extra-virgin olive oil

2 tbsp snipped chives

1. Cook the potatoes in a saucepan of boiling salted water for 20–25 minutes until tender. Drain, then cut in half and leave to cool a little.

2. Meanwhile, bring another saucepan of water to the boil and boil the eggs for 5–6 minutes; add the green beans to the pan 2 minutes before the end of the cooking time. Drain and cool under running water or a bowl of iced water.

3. To make the dressing, whisk the vinegar, mustard and some seasoning together in a salad bowl. Gradually whisk in the oil until you have a glossy dressing. Add the chives and warm potatoes and toss well.

4. Add the beans, tomatoes, tuna, olives and capers to the bowl and toss together. Peel and halve the eggs, add to the top of the salad and serve.

KCALS	FAT	SAT FAT	CARBS	SUGARS	FIBRE	PROTEIN	SALT
350	19.0g	3.0g	23.0g	6.0g	7.0g	19.0g	1.81g

Chinese Chopped Chicken Salad

with Cheat's Bacon XO Sauce

Serves:
4

Equipment:
Frying pan,
small saucepan

Cook's Notes:
XO sauce is a funky chilli and pork sauce that adds a wonderful depth of flavour to Chinese dishes, but it takes time and lots of ingredients to make at home. This is a great little shortcut, using a jar of ready-made bacon jam (easily available online and in supermarkets) and adding a twist with soy sauce, fish sauce and rice vinegar.

350g (12oz) red cabbage (about ⅓), finely shredded

½ Chinese cabbage, shredded

1 large carrot (150g/5oz), peeled and julienned or shredded

2 tbsp sunflower oil

4 boneless, skinless chicken thighs

100g (3½oz) jar bacon jam *(see Cook's Notes)*

2 tsp fish sauce

1 tsp reduced salt soy sauce

2 tsp rice vinegar

1 bird's-eye chilli, finely chopped

For the dressing

2 tbsp rice vinegar

1 tbsp reduced salt soy sauce

1½ tbsp sesame oil

1. Put the shredded cabbages and carrot into a salad bowl. Whisk all the ingredients for the dressing together in a small bowl, pour over the salad and toss to combine. Set aside to soften and macerate.

2. Heat the oil in a frying pan. Season the chicken and fry over a medium heat for 3–4 minutes on each side until just cooked. Set aside to rest.

3. Meanwhile, in a small saucepan warm the bacon jam with the fish sauce, soy sauce, rice vinegar and chilli.

4. Chop the chicken and add to the salad with the warm bacon jam. Toss to combine before serving.

KCALS	FAT	SAT FAT	CARBS	SUGARS	FIBRE	PROTEIN	SALT
317	17.0g	3.0g	20.0g	13.0g	5.0g	17.0g	1.49g

Glossy Turkey Meatballs
with Rice Noodle Salad

Serves:
4

Equipment:
Non-stick sauté
pan with lid

Cook's Notes:
Turkey meat is a great low-fat alternative to pork or lamb when it comes to meatballs and is the perfect partner for the Asian flavours in this recipe.

400g (14oz) turkey mince

1 tbsp reduced salt soy sauce

1 tbsp hoisin sauce

2cm (¾in) piece of ginger, peeled and grated

sunflower oil, for frying

100g (3½oz) vermicelli rice noodles

2 tsp sesame oil

1 tsp rice vinegar

2 large carrots, peeled and shaved into ribbons

1 large courgette, shaved into ribbons

3 spring onions, finely shredded

1. Mix the turkey mince with 1 teaspoon each of soy and hoisin sauce. Add the ginger and plenty of seasoning and shape into 12 meatballs.

2. Heat a little oil in a non-stick sauté pan and fry the meatballs all over for about 5 minutes, until golden. Add the rest of the soy and hoisin and a little splash of water. Cover and steam for 1–2 minutes, then remove the lid and bubble until you have a sticky glaze.

3. Meanwhile, soak the noodles in boiling water for 10 minutes, then drain and cool under cold running water. Tip into a bowl and toss with the sesame oil. Mix the rice vinegar with the carrots and courgette, then toss with the noodles. Serve the noodles with the sticky meatballs, scattered with the spring onions.

KCALS	FAT	SAT FAT	CARBS	SUGARS	FIBRE	PROTEIN	SALT
273	6.0g	1.0g	25.0g	5.0g	3.0g	28.0g	0.67g

BLT Salad

Serves:
4

Equipment:
Large frying pan, slotted spoon

Cook's Notes:
You can easily make your own sun-blushed, also called semi-dried, tomatoes and keep them in oil to have to hand. Roast 300g (10oz) halved cherry tomatoes in a medium oven for 45 minutes until sticky and unctuous. Use them to bring a delicious burst of sweet and tangy colour to dishes.

drizzle of olive oil

200g (7oz) smoked bacon lardons

4 slices of sourdough

1 garlic clove, halved

2 heads of romaine lettuce, leaves separated

150g (5oz) sun-blushed tomatoes

2 tbsp chopped chives

For the dressing

50g (2oz) blue cheese (such as Dolcelatte)

1 tsp red wine vinegar

4 tbsp low-fat natural yoghurt

2 tbsp low-fat mayonnaise

1. Heat a drizzle of oil in a large frying pan and cook the bacon lardons over a medium–high heat for 5–6 minutes until crisp. Remove with a slotted spoon, leaving the bacon fat in the pan.

2. Fry the sourdough in the bacon fat over a medium heat for 1–2 minutes each side until golden, then remove from the pan and rub all over one side with the cut side of garlic clove. Cut into fingers.

3. Toss the lettuce leaves with the crispy bacon, tomatoes and chives on a platter.

4. To make the dressing, use the back of a spoon to blend the blue cheese with the vinegar in a small bowl. Add the yoghurt and mayonnaise and mix to form a smooth dressing. Season well and pour over the salad. Toss the salad gently and serve with the garlic toasts.

KCALS	FAT	SAT FAT	CARBS	SUGARS	FIBRE	PROTEIN	SALT
449	23.0g	7.0g	33.0g	12.0g	11.0g	22.0g	3.10g

Crispy Mushroom, Radicchio & Bacon Salad

(2)

Serves:
4

Equipment:
Frying pan,
slotted spoon,
saucepan

Cook's Notes:
Resist the temptation to move the mushrooms around when you get them in the pan. You want to press them down so they make good contact with the hot fat and then leave to go beautifully crispy. Moving them will cause them to release moisture and steam and not crisp up.

1 tbsp olive oil

200g (7oz) thick-cut smoked bacon lardons or diced pancetta

30g (1oz) unsalted butter

few sprigs of fresh thyme

320g (11¼oz) wild mushrooms (ideally ceps or other European mushroom, but shiitake or oyster would also work)

4 large free-range eggs

450g (1lb) radicchio (about 2 heads), leaves separated

For the dressing

2 tbsp sherry vinegar

1 garlic clove, crushed

3 tbsp extra-virgin olive oil

20g (¾ oz) Parmesan cheese, finely grated

1. Heat the oil in a frying pan and fry the lardons over a medium–high heat for 4–5 minutes until crispy. Transfer to a plate with a slotted spoon, then add the butter and thyme to the bacon fat; once the butter is sizzling add the mushrooms. Fry over a high heat for 5–6 minutes, turning once, until golden and crisp. Season and set aside.

2. Meanwhile, cook the eggs in a saucepan of boiling water for 5–6 minutes. Drain and cool under running water to stop the cooking process, then peel when cool enough to handle.

3. To make the dressing, whisk together the vinegar, garlic and some seasoning, then gradually whisk in the oil. Add half the grated Parmesan to the dressing.

4. Put the radicchio leaves into a salad bowl with the mushrooms and crispy bacon and toss with the dressing. Halve the eggs and serve on top of the salad.

KCALS	FAT	SAT FAT	CARBS	SUGARS	FIBRE	PROTEIN	SALT
414	36.0g	12.0g	2.0g	2.0g	3.0g	20.0g	1.48g

Charred Pork Banh Mi Salad

（3）

Serves:
4

Equipment:
Mini food processor, frying pan or griddle pan

Cook's Notes:
Taking all the flavour of the classic Vietnamese street food sandwich without the heavy bread makes this a great light supper dish.

500g (1lb 2oz) pork tenderloin, thinly sliced

2 tbsp caster sugar

1 tbsp fish sauce

3 garlic cloves

bunch of spring onions, white parts chopped and green parts shredded

3–4 carrots (about 350g/12oz), peeled and julienned or grated

1 red chilli, finely chopped

75ml (1/3 cup) rice wine vinegar

1 romaine lettuce, shredded

½ cucumber, peeled, deseeded and sliced

bunch of coriander, leaves picked

1. Put the pork in a dish. Whizz half the sugar, the fish sauce, garlic and the white parts of the spring onions in a mini food processor with a splash of water to make a paste. Pour over the meat and turn to coat; set aside.

2. Put the carrots and chilli in a small bowl. Heat the rice wine vinegar with an equal amount of water and the rest of the sugar and pour over the top. Set aside.

3. Heat a frying pan or griddle pan over a high heat and cook the pork for about 10 minutes in batches, turning, until lightly charred and cooked through. Set aside to rest.

4. Put the lettuce and cucumber into a salad bowl. Drain the pickled carrots, add to the salad and mix well. Top with the charred pork, coriander leaves and the finely shredded green parts of the spring onions.

KCALS	FAT	SAT FAT	CARBS	SUGARS	FIBRE	PROTEIN	SALT
247	6.0g	2.0g	16.0g	14.0g	8.0g	30.0g	1.34g

Spice-crusted Lamb

with White Bean & Tomato Salad

Serves:
4

Equipment:
Pestle and mortar, ovenproof frying pan

Cook's Notes:
Warm and fragrant and full of the taste of an Italian summer, you could also make this dish with Puy lentils or chickpeas instead of beans.

2 x 150g (5oz) lamb neck fillets

1 tbsp coriander seeds

2 tsp fennel seeds

good pinch of dried chilli flakes

2 tbsp olive oil

500g (1lb 2oz) ripe vine tomatoes, cut into thin wedges

1 x 400g (14oz) tin white beans (such as cannellini or butter beans), drained and rinsed

1 tbsp red wine vinegar

squeeze of lemon juice

2 tbsp extra-virgin olive oil

handful of fresh basil leaves

1. Preheat the oven to 200°C (180°C fan).

2. Put the neck fillets into a dish. Roughly crush the coriander and fennel seeds in a pestle and mortar, then mix with the chilli flakes and half the oil. Press all over the lamb, season well and set aside for 10 minutes.

3. Meanwhile, put the tomatoes and beans on a serving platter. Mix the vinegar and lemon juice with some seasoning, then whisk in the extra-virgin olive oil; pour this over the tomatoes and beans.

4. Heat the remaining tablespoon of olive oil in an ovenproof frying pan and fry the spiced lamb on all sides until sealed and golden all over. Transfer to the oven and cook for 8–10 minutes (the lamb should still be pink in the middle). Rest for 5 minutes, then slice and gently toss through the beans and tomato salad. Scatter with the basil leaves and serve.

KCALS	FAT	SAT FAT	CARBS	SUGARS	FIBRE	PROTEIN	SALT
729	50.0g	14.0g	27.0g	8.0g	11.0g	37.0g	0.39g

Spiced Lamb with Greek Salad

Serves:
3, or
2 generously

Equipment:
Sauté pan

Cook's Notes:
A classic combo to conjure up blue skies, warm sea and Mediterranean holiday sunshine.

1 red onion, very thinly sliced

juice of 1 lemon

300g (10oz) lamb leg steaks (about 2–3 steaks)

2 tbsp fresh oregano leaves

pinch of chilli flakes

2 tbsp olive oil

2 tbsp extra-virgin olive oil

1 romaine lettuce, shredded

½ cucumber, peeled, deseeded and chopped

8 small vine tomatoes, chopped

75g (2½oz) black olives, halved

125g (4½oz) feta cheese, crumbled

1. Toss the onion with half the lemon juice and some salt and pepper and set aside to lightly pickle.

2. Put the lamb in a bowl with the oregano, chilli flakes and olive oil. Season well. Place a sauté pan over a medium–high heat and fry the lamb for 3–4 minutes on each side until medium rare. Allow to rest for 5 minutes before slicing thinly.

3. In a bowl, use a fork to blend the remaining lemon juice with some salt and pepper and the extra-virgin olive oil. Add the lettuce, pickled onion, cucumber, tomatoes and olives and toss to combine, then gently stir through the feta.

4. Serve the salad topped with the sliced lamb.

KCALS	FAT	SAT FAT	CARBS	SUGARS	FIBRE	PROTEIN	SALT
512	35.0g	12.0g	13.0g	12.0g	9.0g	31.0g	2.08g

Soy & Sesame Steak Noodle Salad

Serves:
2

Equipment:
Saucepan,
frying pan
with lid

Cook's Notes:
A quick and satisfying Asian beef and noodle salad
packed with flavour.

250g (9oz) sirloin or
rib eye steak

2 tbsp sunflower oil

3 tbsp reduced salt soy sauce

1 tbsp toasted sesame seeds

150g (5oz) dried udon noodles

1 tbsp sesame oil

4 baby pak choi, quartered

2 large carrots, peeled and
shaved into ribbons

1½ tbsp rice wine vinegar

handful of coriander leaves

handful of mint leaves

1. Put the steak in a dish with 1 tablespoon of the sunflower oil, 1 tablespoon of the soy sauce half the sesame seeds. Set aside for 5 minutes.

2. Cook the noodles in a saucepan of boiling water for 3–4 minutes, then drain and toss with 1 teaspoon of the sesame oil.

3. Place a frying pan over a high heat until it is as hot as possible and fry the steak for 1–2 minutes each side until charred on the outside but still rare. Set aside to rest for 5 minutes.

4. Toss the vegetables in the rest of the sunflower oil. Return the frying pan to the high heat and quickly toss the vegetables in it to soften them slightly. Add a splash of water and cover to let them steam for 1–2 minutes, then combine with the drained noodles, the rice wine vinegar and the rest of the sesame oil and soy sauce.

5. Slice the steak. Top the noodles with slices of steak, plenty of herbs and the rest of the sesame seeds.

KCALS	FAT	SAT FAT	CARBS	SUGARS	FIBRE	PROTEIN	SALT
783	34.0g	8.0g	75.0g	17.0g	8.0g	41.0g	4.63g

Steak with Blistered Summer Vegetables

& Fish Sauce Dressing

Serves:	**Equipment:**	**Cook's Notes:**
4	Griddle pan	If the weather is good, try cooking this on the barbecue rather than indoors to give it that lovely smoky flavour.

450g (1lb) sirloin steak, excess fat trimmed

olive oil or groundnut oil, to drizzle

1 tbsp fish sauce

2 baby gem lettuces, quartered

bunch of spring onions, trimmed

bunch of asparagus, woody ends snapped off

2 courgettes, thinly sliced lengthways

bunch of coriander, leaves picked

2 tbsp roasted peanuts, roughly chopped

For the dressing

juice of 1 lime

1 tbsp fish sauce

1 tsp caster sugar

2 tbsp olive or groundnut oil

1 tbsp sesame oil

1. Put the steak in a dish with a drizzle of oil, the fish sauce and plenty of black pepper. Set aside.

2. Place a griddle pan over a high heat. Toss the vegetables in a little oil, then griddle them for 2–3 minutes on all sides, or until lightly charred. Tip into a serving dish.

3. Remove the steak from the marinade, add to the pan and griddle for 1–2 minutes each side. Remove from the pan and set aside to rest.

4. To make the dressing, put the lime juice, fish sauce and sugar into a bowl and whisk until the sugar has dissolved, then whisk in the oils.

5. Slice the steak into generous slices and arrange on top of the griddled veggies. Scatter with the coriander leaves and peanuts, drizzle over the dressing and serve.

KCALS	FAT	SAT FAT	CARBS	SUGARS	FIBRE	PROTEIN	SALT
377	25.0g	7.0g	6.0g	5.0g	5.0g	29.0g	1.57g

Bowl Food

When all that will do is a warm bowl of comfort and nourishment, this collection of recipes will fill the void. Soups, stews, curries and everything in between, these recipes rely heavily on vegetables and a pep of spice and heat to leave you with simple satisfaction.

Spiced Carrot & Coriander Soup

Serves:
4 (makes 1.3 litres/2 pints)

Equipment:
Saucepan, hand-held stick blender or food processor

Cook's Notes:
Fresh turmeric has a livelier flavour than the ground spice and its nutrients are more easily absorbed by the body, so look out for it in big supermarkets and ethnic food shops.

2 tbsp vegetable or groundnut oil

1 small onion, finely chopped

1 lemongrass stalk, bashed with the back of a knife

3cm (1¼in) piece of ginger, peeled and grated

small finger of fresh turmeric, peeled and grated (or use 1 tsp ground turmeric)

1 red chilli, deseeded and finely chopped

700g (1½lb) carrots, peeled and chopped

1 x 400ml (14fl oz) tin reduced fat coconut milk

1 tbsp fish sauce

juice of 1 lime, plus wedges to serve

handful of coriander, chopped, plus a few leaves to garnish

1. Heat the oil in a large saucepan and fry the onion with the lemongrass over a medium heat until it has softened. Add the ginger, turmeric and chilli and fry for 1 minute, then add the carrots and mix well.

2. Add the coconut milk and 900ml (3¾ cups) water from a just-boiled kettle. Bring to the boil, then reduce the heat and simmer for 20 minutes until the carrots are tender. Remove and discard the lemongrass, add the fish sauce and blitz with a hand-held stick blender until smooth (or transfer to a food processor).

3. Season to taste with lime juice and stir through the chopped coriander. Serve garnished with coriander leaves and lime wedges on the side.

KCALS	FAT	SAT FAT	CARBS	SUGARS	FIBRE	PROTEIN	SALT
195	14.0g	8.0g	13.0g	10.0g	5.0g	2.0g	1.12g

Super Green Spinach, Pea & Mint Soup

(2) (V)

Serves:
6, or 4
generously

Equipment:
Saucepan,
hand-held stick
blender or food
processor

Cook's Notes:
As well as being a well-known source of iron, spinach,
like all brassicas, is a nutritional powerhouse, packed
with vitamins A, C and K.

2 tbsp olive oil

bunch of spring onions,
chopped

500g (1lb 2oz) baby spinach

300g (10oz) frozen peas

200g (7oz) broccoli florets

1.2 litres (5 cups)
vegetable stock

handful of mint leaves

150g (5oz) feta cheese,
crumbled

1. Heat the oil in a saucepan and gently fry the spring onions
   for 5 minutes over a medium heat until softened.

2. Add the spinach, peas and broccoli and pour over the stock.
   Bring to the boil and season with salt and pepper, then reduce
   the heat and simmer for 10 minutes until the veg is tender.

3. Add most of the mint leaves and blitz until smooth, either
   using a hand-held stick blender or by transferring to a food
   processor. Serve topped with mint leaves and a scattering
   of feta.

COOK'S TIP

Keep it veggie:
check the packaging
on the feta to make
sure it is vegetarian.

KCALS	FAT	SAT FAT	CARBS	SUGARS	FIBRE	PROTEIN	SALT
185	11.0g	4.0g	8.0g	5.0g	6.0g	11.0g	0.79g

Cauliflower Soup with Cumin & Basil Oil

(2) (V)

Serves:
2 generously

Equipment:
Large saucepan,
hand-held stick
blender or
blender

Cook's Notes:
It's worthwhile making a larger batch of the basil oil used
in this recipe as it keeps brilliantly in the fridge for up to
one week. Use to drizzle over tomato salads, roast vegetables
or grilled salmon.

2 tbsp olive oil

1 large onion, finely chopped

1 garlic clove, crushed

1 tbsp cumin seeds

1 large cauliflower,
cut into florets

300ml (1¼ cups)
semi-skimmed milk

300ml (1¼ cups)
vegetable stock

3 tbsp ground almonds

squeeze of lemon juice

large bunch of basil,
leaves picked

50ml extra-virgin olive oil

1. Heat the olive oil in a large saucepan and gently fry the
   onion over a low heat for 10 minutes. Add the garlic and
   all but a pinch of the cumin seeds and fry for 30 seconds,
   then add the cauliflower and stir to coat in the oil. Add the
   milk and stock, season with salt and pepper and bring to
   the boil. Reduce the heat and simmer for about 15 minutes
   until tender.

2. Strain off the liquid and use a hand-held stick blender or
   blender to blitz the cauliflower together with the ground
   almonds, adding back enough of the liquid until you have
   a lovely thick consistency. Check the seasoning and add a
   squeeze of lemon juice to taste. If you like it a little looser
   you can add an extra splash of milk or water.

3. Meanwhile, finely chop the basil leaves, add to a small
   bowl and stir in the extra-virgin olive oil. Alternatively,
   place the basil leaves and oil in a mini food processor
   and blitz until smooth.

4. Serve the soup in bowls with a drizzle of basil oil and
   a scattering of cumin seeds.

KCALS	FAT	SAT FAT	CARBS	SUGARS	FIBRE	PROTEIN	SALT
558	35.0g	6.0g	32.0g	25.0g	12.0g	22.0g	0.32g

Thai Green Curry Noodle Soup

(2) (VG)

Serves:	Equipment:	Cook's Notes:
4	Saucepan	Super-quick and easy to make, this fragrant Thai soup hits the spot for a great midweek supper.

1 tbsp sunflower oil

3 tbsp green curry paste

2 aubergines, cubed

1 x 400ml (14fl oz) tin reduced fat coconut milk

400ml (1¾ cups) vegetable stock

300g (10oz) tenderstem broccoli, trimmed

170g (6oz) sugar snap peas

100g (3½oz) vermicelli rice noodles

2 spring onions, finely chopped

handful of coriander, leaves picked

1 red chilli, thinly sliced

lime wedges, to serve

1. Heat the oil in a saucepan. Fry the curry paste over a medium–high heat for 1–2 minutes, then add the aubergines and cook slowly for 10 minutes until nearly tender. Add the coconut milk and vegetable stock, and bring to the boil, then add the green veg and simmer for 3–4 minutes.

2. Meanwhile, soak the rice noodles in a bowl of boiling water for 10 minutes. Drain and rinse under cold water to stop them cooking further.

3. Divide the noodles between four bowls and pour over the soup. Scatter with the spring onions, coriander leaves and chilli and serve with lime wedges for squeezing over the top.

COOK'S TIP

Keep it vegan: make sure the vegetable stock does not contain milk derivatives.

KCALS	FAT	SAT FAT	CARBS	SUGARS	FIBRE	PROTEIN	SALT
310	14.0g	7.0g	31.0g	8.0g	10.0g	9.0g	0.73g

Chilli, Coconut, Sweet Potato & Split Pea Soup

(2) (VG)

Serves:
6, or 4 generously

Equipment:
Large saucepan, hand-held stick blender or food processor

Cook's Notes:
This warming curry-style soup is packed with hearty goodness and velvety sweet coconut.

4 tbsp sunflower oil

2 red onions, finely chopped

1 tsp ground coriander

1 tsp cumin seeds

1 tsp chilli flakes, plus extra to garnish

600g (1lb 5oz) sweet potatoes, peeled and diced

250g (9oz) yellow split peas

1 x 400ml (14fl oz) tin reduced fat coconut milk

1.5 litres (6 cups) vegetable stock, plus more if needed

1. Heat 1 tablespoon of the oil in a large saucepan, add the onions and allow to soften over a low heat for 5 minutes. Add the ground coriander, cumin seeds and chilli flakes and fry for about 1 minute before adding the sweet potatoes and the split peas.

2. Pour over the coconut milk and stock and season with salt and pepper. Bring to the boil and cook for 10 minutes, then reduce the heat and simmer gently for 15 minutes until tender.

3. Use a hand-held stick blender or food processor to blitz until smooth, adding more stock if needed. Garnish with a scattering of chilli flakes and serve.

COOK'S TIP

Keep it vegan: make sure the vegetable stock does not contain milk derivatives.

KCALS	FAT	SAT FAT	CARBS	SUGARS	FIBRE	PROTEIN	SALT
399	15.0g	5.0g	48.0g	15.0g	9.0g	13.0g	0.22g

Egg, Shiitake & Dark Greens Ramen

(2) (V)

Serves:
4

Equipment:
3 saucepans

Cook's Notes:
If you have extra time, try marinating the boiled eggs in a 2:1 mix of soy sauce to mirin, plus a dash of sake. Peel them and place in a bowl of this marinade for a couple of hours to take on a deep, rich flavour and colour.

2 tbsp sunflower oil

3 garlic cloves, thinly sliced

1 heaped tbsp brown (or red) miso paste

750ml (3 cups) vegetable stock

320g (11¼oz) shiitake mushrooms, halved if large

320g (11¼oz) shredded cavolo nero or kale (remove tough stalks first)

1 tbsp reduced salt soy sauce

1 tbsp sesame oil

4 large free-range eggs

200g (7oz) dried ramen noodles

1 sheet of dried nori, thinly sliced

1. Heat the sunflower oil in a saucepan and gently fry the garlic for 30 seconds. Add the miso paste and vegetable stock and bring to the boil. Add the mushrooms and greens and simmer gently for 10 minutes, then add the soy sauce and sesame oil.

2. Bring a saucepan of water to the boil, lower in the eggs and cook for 5–6 minutes, then drain and cool in a bowl of ice-cold water until they are cool enough to peel.

3. Cook the noodles in a saucepan of salted boiling water for 2–3 minutes. Drain and divide between four bowls. Add the eggs to the broth for a minute just to warm them through, then divide the eggs, greens, mushrooms and broth between the bowls. Top with the nori and serve.

KCALS	FAT	SAT FAT	CARBS	SUGARS	FIBRE	PROTEIN	SALT
437	16.0g	3.0g	49.0g	4.0g	6.0g	20.0g	1.64g

Soy Multigrain Porridge

with Crispy Chilli Eggs

Serves:
4

Equipment:
Saucepan,
non-stick deep
frying pan

Cook's Notes:
Savoury porridge is just as warming and hearty as the
more usual breakfast variety. Make lovely, crisp, curly
spring onions as a garnish: shred the onions lengthways and
place in a bowl of iced water for 10–20 minutes.

200g (7oz) multigrain
porridge (such as oats,
quinoa, millet)

850ml (3½ cups)
vegetable stock

1 tbsp reduced salt soy sauce

125ml (½ cup) sunflower oil

4 large free-range eggs

2 tsp sesame oil

2 tbsp oyster sauce

1 red chilli, very thinly sliced

5 spring onions, shredded
lengthways *(see Cook's Notes)*

handful of coriander leaves

1. Put the porridge and stock into a saucepan and bring to
a simmer. Cook gently for 12–15 minutes until you have
a fragrant porridge. Add the soy sauce and set aside.

2. Heat the sunflower oil in a non-stick frying pan over quite
a high heat. Add the eggs and allow the whites to bubble and
crisp up. As soon as the whites are set, the edges crispy and
the yolks are cooked but still a bit runny, remove from the
pan and drain on kitchen paper.

3. Divide the porridge between four bowls and top each with
an egg. Drizzle with the sesame oil and oyster sauce and
scatter with the red chilli, spring onions and coriander
leaves. Serve straight away.

KCALS	FAT	SAT FAT	CARBS	SUGARS	FIBRE	PROTEIN	SALT
383	18.0g	3.0g	35.0g	1.0g	5.0g	17.0g	1.47g

Sumac Fried Eggs with Persian Rice

Serves:
6

Equipment:
Saucepan with lid, small saucepan, frying pan

Cook's Notes:
Lemony sumac adds a little zing to this herby rice.

250g (9oz) basmati rice

200g (7oz) frozen or fresh broad beans

2 tbsp extra-virgin olive oil

handful of coriander, chopped

small bunch of dill, finely chopped

small bunch of flat-leaf parsley, finely chopped

200g (7oz) natural yoghurt

2 tbsp tahini

2 tbsp olive oil

6 large free-range eggs

good sprinkle of sumac

100g (3½ oz) flaked almonds, toasted

1. Wash the rice and put into a saucepan with 300ml (1¼ cups) cold salted water. Cover and bring to the boil, then reduce the heat and simmer gently for 12 minutes. Turn off the heat and leave to stand with the lid on for 5 minutes.

2. Bring a small saucepan of water to the boil and blanch the broad beans for 2 minutes. Drain and refresh under cold water. You can double pod them if you have time to reveal the bright green insides.

3. Uncover the rice, fluff up with a fork and tip into a serving bowl. Allow to cool a little, then stir in the beans, extra-virgin olive oil and herbs.

4. Mix the yoghurt and tahini together with some seasoning.

5. Heat the olive oil in a frying pan and fry the eggs for 2–3 minutes until just set – spoon a little of the hot oil over the top of the yolks just to set them slightly. Serve the eggs on top of the rice with a dollop of tahini yoghurt, a good sprinkling of sumac and a scattering of flaked almonds.

KCALS	FAT	SAT FAT	CARBS	SUGARS	FIBRE	PROTEIN	SALT
482	27.0g	4.0g	35.0g	4.0g	4.0g	21.0g	0.37g

Salmon Poke Bowl

Serves:
4

Equipment:
Saucepan
with lid

Cook's Notes:
Salmon works brilliantly in place of the more traditional tuna in this Hawaiian classic poke bowl – plus it's much more friendly on the wallet.

225g (8oz) sushi rice

2 tbsp reduced salt soy sauce

1 tbsp mirin

pinch of chilli flakes

2 tsp sesame oil

generous pinch of sugar

500g (1lb 2oz) sashimi-grade salmon, diced

1 avocado, sliced

3 spring onions, thinly sliced

1 tbsp white and black sesame seeds

1. Rinse the sushi rice really well, changing the water a few times until it no longer runs milky-white. Fill a saucepan with 350ml (1½ cups) cold salted water and add the rice. Bring to the boil, then reduce the heat and simmer gently for 10 minutes, or according to the packet instructions. Remove from the heat, cover and set aside for 10 minutes, then fluff up with a fork and leave to cool slightly.

2. Use a fork to blend the soy sauce with the mirin, chilli flakes, sesame oil and sugar. Pour over the salmon and let stand for no more than 5 minutes.

3. Divide the just-warm rice between four bowls. Top with the salmon, avocado and spring onions. Scatter with the black and white sesame seeds and serve.

KCALS	FAT	SAT FAT	CARBS	SUGARS	FIBRE	PROTEIN	SALT
548	25.0g	5.0g	48.0g	2.0g	3.0g	34.0g	0.87g

Chickpea Stew
with Chermoula

Serves:
4

Equipment:
Large saucepan

Cook's Notes:
Chermoula is a gloriously vibrant green herb paste from North Africa, full of lemon, coriander, garlic and chilli.

3 tbsp olive oil

2 onions, finely chopped

2 garlic cloves, thinly sliced

1 x 460g (1lb) jar roasted red peppers, drained and sliced

1 x 400g (14oz) tin chopped tomatoes

2 x 400g (14oz) tins chickpeas, drained and rinsed

400ml (1¾ cups) vegetable stock

3 large handfuls (about 120g/4oz) of baby spinach

handful of coriander leaves, roughly chopped

2–3 tbsp chermoula paste

1. Heat the oil in a large saucepan and gently fry the onions for 6–8 minutes until softened. Add the garlic and cook for 30 seconds, then add the roasted red peppers, tomatoes, chickpeas and stock.

2. Season with salt and pepper and cook for 20 minutes over a medium–high heat until rich and thickened. Add the spinach and allow to wilt, then stir in most of the coriander leaves and chermoula.

3. Serve with an extra drizzle of chermoula paste and a sprinkling of coriander.

KCALS	FAT	SAT FAT	CARBS	SUGARS	FIBRE	PROTEIN	SALT
341	15.0g	2.0g	32.0g	8.0g	10.0g	15.0g	0.80g

Italian Bean Stew

(3)

Serves:	Equipment:	Cook's Notes:
4	Large saucepan	This simple dish is rich and satisfying. Don't be put off by the anchovies – they melt into the stew and just add a rich, salty note to the end flavour.

2 tbsp olive oil

1 large onion, thinly sliced

2 celery sticks, finely chopped

2 garlic cloves, crushed

3 anchovies, chopped

4–5 sprigs of fresh thyme, leaves picked

500g (1lb 2oz) spring greens, shredded

1 litre (4 cups) vegetable or chicken stock

2 x 400g (14oz) tins cannellini beans, drained and rinsed

100g (3½oz) watercress

extra-virgin olive oil, to drizzle

30g (1oz) Parmesan shavings, to serve

1. Heat the olive oil in a saucepan and gently fry the onion and celery for 10 minutes until softened.

2. Add the garlic, anchovies and thyme and cook for 1 minute before adding the spring greens and stock. Season well, bring to the boil, then reduce the heat and simmer for 10 minutes.

3. Add the beans and watercress and cook for 5 minutes more. Serve with a good drizzle of extra-virgin olive oil and a few Parmesan shavings.

KCALS	FAT	SAT FAT	CARBS	SUGARS	FIBRE	PROTEIN	SALT
317	10.0g	3.0g	28.0g	6.0g	14.0g	22.0g	2.0g

Easy Red Lentil Dahl

Serves:
4

Equipment:
Saucepan,
small frying pan

Cook's Notes:
A gloriously golden orange bowl of warming comfort.

4 tbsp olive oil

1 large onion, finely chopped

2 garlic cloves, crushed

1 tbsp cumin seeds

1 tbsp black mustard seeds

2 tsp ground turmeric

1 tsp chilli powder

250g (9oz) red lentils, rinsed well

1 x 400g (14oz) tin chopped tomatoes

1 x 400ml tin (14fl oz) reduced fat coconut milk

large handful of chopped coriander

1. Heat half the oil in a saucepan and gently fry the onion for 5 minutes until softened. Add the garlic, 2 teaspoons of the cumin seeds and 2 teaspoons of the mustard seeds and fry for 30 seconds until the mustard seeds start to pop.

2. Stir in the ground spices, allowing them to become aromatic before adding the lentils, tomatoes and coconut milk. Season with salt and pepper and simmer for 25 minutes, adding a splash more water if you need to, until the lentils are tender.

3. Heat the remaining oil in a small frying pan over a medium–high heat. Add the rest of the cumin and mustard seeds and cook for 20 seconds. Serve the dahl topped with a drizzle of the spiced oil and lots of fresh coriander. The remaining oil will keep in the fridge for up to a week.

KCALS	FAT	SAT FAT	CARBS	SUGARS	FIBRE	PROTEIN	SALT
823	33.0g	15.0g	88.0g	19.0g	14.0g	37.0g	0.32g

Chickpea & Greens Tagine

(4) (VG)

Serves:
4

Equipment:
Casserole or
deep sauté pan
with lid

Cook's Notes:
This speedy 'tagine' falls somewhere in between a French
ratatouille and a Moroccan tagine. It's a wonderful recipe
for using up any stray vegetables that you may find lurking
at the bottom of your fridge.

2 tbsp olive oil

2 red onions, thinly sliced

2 tsp ras el hanout

3 garlic cloves, crushed

1 large fennel bulb,
thinly sliced

2 medium courgettes, diced

1 red pepper, deseeded
and sliced

250g (9oz) chopped fresh
vine tomatoes

1 x 400g (14oz) tin chickpeas,
drained and rinsed

200g (7oz) spring greens,
finely shredded

handful of flat-leaf parsley,
finely chopped

1. Heat the oil in a lidded casserole or deep sauté pan.
   Gently fry the onions over a low heat for 6–8 minutes
   until softened. Add the ras el hanout and garlic, cook
   for 1 minute, then add the fennel and courgettes.

2. Increase the heat to high and cook for 5 minutes before
   adding the red pepper, tomatoes and chickpeas along with
   400ml (1¾ cups) water from a just-boiled kettle. Season
   well, cover and simmer for 15 minutes.

3. Add the spring greens, cover and cook for a few more
   minutes until they are just wilted. Scatter with the
   parsley and serve.

KCALS	FAT	SAT FAT	CARBS	SUGARS	FIBRE	PROTEIN	SALT
222	8.0g	1.0g	21.0g	10.0g	12.0g	9.0g	0.24g

Aubergine Curry with Turmeric Cauliflower Rice

(4) (V)

Serves:
4

Equipment:
Large sauté pan, coarse box grater (optional), saucepan

Cook's Notes:
Aubergines are fantastic flavour carriers, making them perfect for veggie curries. Cauliflower rice is easy to make at home: either pulse the cauliflower in a food processor, or coarsely grate, until it resembles grains of rice.

3 tbsp olive oil

1 large onion, finely chopped

2 garlic cloves, crushed

2.5cm (1in) piece of ginger, peeled and grated

3 aubergines, cubed

2 tsp nigella seeds or black mustard seeds

2 tsp garam masala

1 x 400g (14oz) tin chopped tomatoes

200g (7oz) natural yoghurt, plus extra to serve

For the cauliflower rice

1 tbsp olive oil

1 garlic clove, crushed

1 tsp ground turmeric

800g (1lb 12oz) riced cauliflower *(shop-bought or see Cook's Notes)*

1. Heat half the oil in a large sauté pan and gently fry the onion for 6 minutes until softened. Add the garlic and ginger and fry for 1 minute, then add the rest of the oil and the aubergines. Increase the heat and brown the aubergines on all sides.

2. Add the nigella (or mustard) seeds, garam masala, tomatoes and plenty of seasoning, reduce the heat and bubble for 15 minutes until the aubergine is lovely and tender and the sauce has thickened.

3. Meanwhile, prepare the cauliflower rice: heat the oil in a saucepan and fry the garlic and turmeric for 30 seconds, then add the riced cauliflower and a splash of water. Cover and steam for 5 minutes until hot and tender. Season well.

4. Stir the yoghurt through the curry and allow to simmer gently for 1–2 minutes. Serve with the cauliflower rice and an extra dollop of yoghurt.

KCALS	FAT	SAT FAT	CARBS	SUGARS	FIBRE	PROTEIN	SALT
310	16.0g	3.0g	24.0g	20.0g	12.0g	11.0g	0.17g

Lighter Dan Dan Noodles

Serves:
4

Equipment:
Frying pan,
saucepan,
slotted spoon

Cook's Notes:
This is a super-light version of the classic Sichuan street food dish that usually uses minced pork.

2 tsp Szechuan peppercorns, lightly crushed

2 tbsp sunflower oil

2.5cm (1in) piece of ginger, peeled and grated

400g (14oz) soya mince

250g (9oz) Chinese greens such as pak choi or choi sum, halved or quartered

4 spring onions, thinly sliced

1 tbsp Shaoxing rice wine

3 tbsp reduced salt soy sauce

400g (14oz) ramen noodles

1 tbsp rice wine vinegar

2 tbsp chilli oil

1. Toast the Szechuan peppercorns in a dry frying pan for 1 minute, then set aside. Add the oil to the pan and fry the ginger for 1–2 minutes, then add the soya mince and toasted peppercorns. Fry until the mince is crisp and dry.

2. Blanch the greens in a saucepan of boiling water, then remove from the water with a slotted spoon, leaving the water to cook your noodles with. Add the greens to the mince and toss well, before adding the spring onions, rice wine and 1 tablespoon of the soy sauce.

3. Cook the noodles in the boiling water for 2–3 minutes, then drain and divide between four bowls. Mix the rest of the soy sauce with the rice wine vinegar and chilli oil. Divide the greens and mince over the noodles, drizzle with the chilli sauce and serve.

KCALS	FAT	SAT FAT	CARBS	SUGARS	FIBRE	PROTEIN	SALT
590	13.0g	2.0g	84.0g	7.0g	11.0g	28.0g	1.69g

Mushroom Grain Bowl

with Harissa & Quick Fried Kale

Serves:
4

Equipment:
Large frying pan

Cook's Notes:
This is a fabulously filling veggie supper to satisfy even the most diehard of meat-eaters.

30g (1oz) unsalted butter

2 tbsp olive oil

600g (1lb 5oz) oyster mushrooms, torn if large

2 garlic cloves, thinly sliced

1 tsp each hot smoked and sweet smoked paprika, plus a pinch to serve

320g (11¼oz) kale, tough stems removed and leaves roughly chopped

2 x 250g (9oz) sachets cooked mixed grains (such as freekeh, pearl barley, quinoa, wheatberries)

2 tbsp extra-virgin olive oil

2 tbsp chopped dill

3 tbsp chopped parsley

good squeeze of lemon juice

4 dollops of low-fat soured cream

1. Heat the butter and half the olive oil in a large frying pan over a medium–high heat. Add the mushrooms and cook on one side, pressing down, until really crispy. Turn over, add the garlic and cook the other side, again until golden. You may need to do this in batches if you don't have a big enough pan. Add the paprika, season well with salt and pepper and set aside in a bowl.

2. Heat the remaining oil in the pan, add the kale and fry for 3–4 minutes until softened. Season with lots of black pepper and toss with the mushrooms.

3. Heat the grains according to the packet instructions and mix with the extra-virgin olive oil, herbs and lemon juice to taste. Divide the grains between four bowls and add the mushrooms and kale. Top each bowl with a dollop of soured cream and a sprinkle of smoked paprika and serve.

KCALS	FAT	SAT FAT	CARBS	SUGARS	FIBRE	PROTEIN	SALT
484	28.0g	9.0g	40.0g	2.0g	9.0g	14.0g	0.48g

Chickpea Pasta with Cauliflower Bolognese

②

Serves:
6, or 4
generously

Equipment:
Food processor,
sauté pan,
saucepan

Cook's Notes:
If you don't have a food processor you can coarsely grate
the cauliflower instead. Chickpea pasta is one of the best
and most delicious gluten-free alternatives to regular pasta,
but if you wanted you could use wholemeal pasta instead.

650g (1lb 7oz) cauliflower,
broken into florets

250g (9oz) chestnut
mushrooms, finely chopped

3 tbsp olive oil

1 onion, finely chopped

3 garlic cloves, crushed

good pinch of chilli flakes

2 sprigs of rosemary, leaves
stripped and finely chopped

3 tbsp tomato purée

300g (10oz) chickpea pasta

40g (1½oz) Parmesan cheese,
finely grated

1. In a food processor, blitz the cauliflower until it is riced and
tip into a bowl. Add the mushrooms to the food processor
and pulse these too until they are chopped small.

2. Heat the oil in a large sauté pan and fry the onion for
5 minutes over a medium heat until soft, then add the
garlic, chilli flakes and rosemary and fry for 30 seconds.
Add the cauliflower and mushrooms, season well with
salt and pepper and fry over a high heat for 6–7 minutes.
Add the tomato purée and cook for a few more minutes.

3. Meanwhile, cook the pasta in a saucepan of boiling salted
water for 10 minutes. Drain, reserving 250ml (1 cup) of
the water. Add the pasta to the cauliflower pan and toss
together with half the Parmesan for 2–3 minutes, loosen
with the reserved pasta cooking water as needed. Serve
with the rest of the Parmesan scattered over the top.

COOK'S TIP

Make it veggie:
swap the Parmesan
for a vegetarian
alternative.

KCALS	FAT	SAT FAT	CARBS	SUGARS	FIBRE	PROTEIN	SALT
318	11.0g	3.0g	34.0g	7.0g	8.0g	17.0g	0.16g

Thai-style Aubergine with Mint & Jasmine Rice

Serves:
4

Equipment:
Saucepan

Cook's Notes:
You really won't miss the meat at all in this filling bowl of super-tender aubergines in a rich sticky sauce.

2 large aubergines, sliced into fingers about 2cm (¾in) thick

2 garlic cloves, crushed

2 Thai red chillies, deseeded and finely chopped

100ml (½ cup) reduced salt soy sauce

1 tbsp brown sugar

1 tbsp fish sauce

1 tbsp olive oil

300g (10oz) jasmine rice

juice of 1 lime

handful of small young mint leaves

2 tbsp roasted peanuts

1. Put the aubergines into a dish. Use a fork to blend the garlic, chillies, soy sauce, sugar, fish sauce and half the oil together in a small bowl until smooth. Pour this over the aubergine fingers to coat them and leave to marinate (if you have the time) for at least 10 minutes.

2. Cook the rice according to the packet instructions.

3. Heat the remaining oil in a large non-stick frying pan. Remove the aubergine fingers from the marinade and slowly fry for 10 minutes over a medium heat until very tender and browned. Add the rest of marinade to the pan and cook until sticky. Add the lime juice to taste.

4. Spoon the rice into bowls and top with the sticky aubergine. Scatter with the mint leaves and peanuts and serve.

KCALS	FAT	SAT FAT	CARBS	SUGARS	FIBRE	PROTEIN	SALT
459	8.0g	1.0g	80.0g	11.0g	7.0g	12.0g	3.42g

Vietnamese Turmeric & Dill Fish *with Rice Noodles*

Serves:
4

Equipment:
Wok or
frying pan

Cook's Notes:
Sunshine yellow deliciousness with a hit of chilli and herbs,
this unusual Vietnamese dish is best enjoyed in Hanoi.
However, if you can't get to Vietnam in time for dinner,
you can take inspiration from this wonderful cuisine with
a speedy and altogether different fish supper.

2 tsp ground turmeric

3cm (1¼in) piece of ginger,
peeled and grated

1 tsp caster sugar

2 tbsp fish sauce

500g (1lb 2oz) sustainable
cod loin, cut into chunks

100g (3½ oz) vermicelli
rice noodles

60ml (¼ cup) sunflower oil

1 red chilli, finely chopped

large handful of dill fronds

large handful of
coriander leaves

bunch of spring onions,
shredded

2–3 tbsp unsalted roasted
peanuts, chopped

1. Mix the turmeric with the ginger, sugar and fish sauce in a
shallow dish to make a quick marinade. Toss the fish in the
marinade and set aside for 5–10 minutes while you prepare
the noodles.

2. Soak the noodles in boiling water for 10 minutes.

3. Meanwhile, heat the oil in a wok or frying pan and fry the
fish over a high heat for 3–4 minutes until just cooked.
Turn the fish carefully so it doesn't break. Remove from
the heat and add the chilli, herbs and spring onions and
lightly toss together.

4. Drain the noodles and divide between four bowls. Add the
chilli-herb fish pieces, scatter with the peanuts and serve.

KCALS	FAT	SAT FAT	CARBS	SUGARS	FIBRE	PROTEIN	SALT
383	20.0g	3.0g	23.0g	2.0g	2.0g	28.0g	2.41g

Angry Chicken

Serves:
4

Equipment:
Wok, slotted spoon

Cook's Notes:
A fiery chicken dish worth seeking spicy red Thai chillies to deliver a serious punch of heat.

4 skinless chicken breasts, diced

1 tbsp reduced salt soy sauce

2 tbsp cornflour

1 large free-range egg

2 tbsp sunflower oil

2 small red chillies, thinly sliced

2 peppers (1 red, 1 green), deseeded and sliced

2 medium courgettes, cut into batons

For the sauce

300ml (1¼ cups) chicken stock

2 tbsp reduced salt soy sauce

4 tbsp rice vinegar

2 tbsp tomato purée

1 tbsp caster sugar

2 tsp cornflour

1. Toss the chicken pieces in a bowl with the soy sauce. In a separate bowl, whisk the cornflour and egg together to form a batter.

2. Heat the oil in a wok. Dip the chicken into the batter and fry over a high heat for 4–5 minutes until golden and crisp and just cooked. Scoop out with a slotted spoon and set aside on a plate lined with kitchen paper.

3. Add the chillies and peppers to the pan and fry for 3–4 minutes before adding all the sauce ingredients, except for the cornflour. Simmer over a high heat for 5 minutes, then blend 2–3 tablespoons of the sauce with the remaining cornflour in a cup until smooth. Return to the pan and bubble until the sauce thickens.

4. Return the chicken to the pan and simmer for 2–3 minutes until the chicken is sticky and coated. Serve in deep bowls.

5. Meanwhile steam the courgette batons for 2–3 minutes, then divide between four bowls. Serve with the hot and sour chicken.

KCALS	FAT	SAT FAT	CARBS	SUGARS	FIBRE	PROTEIN	SALT
382	13.0g	1.0g	21.0g	11.0g	3.0g	44.0g	1.71g

Chicken Dumpling & Spring Vegetable Soup

Serves:
4

Equipment:
Food processor, large saucepan

Cook's Notes:
Blitzing the chicken gives it a springy texture that holds together brilliantly as a dumpling, absorbing all the flavours of this ultra fresh-tasting soup.

4 chicken breasts, roughly chopped

2 garlic cloves, crushed

handful of chopped flat-leaf parsley

2 tbsp snipped chives

50g (2oz) plain flour

good grating of fresh nutmeg

1 litre (4 cups) fresh, low-salt chicken stock

150g (5oz) baby carrots, trimmed

150g (5oz) spring greens, shredded

150g (5oz) tenderstem broccoli, trimmed

1. Blitz the chicken in a food processor with the garlic and plenty of seasoning. Tip into a bowl and add the herbs, flour and nutmeg. Mix well and shape into 16 balls each about the size of a walnut.

2. Heat the stock in a large saucepan. Add the carrots and chicken dumplings and cook for 3–4 minutes. Add the spring greens and broccoli, cover and cook for 5 minutes more until the veg is tender and the chicken cooked. Season to taste with salt and pepper before serving in bowls.

KCALS	FAT	SAT FAT	CARBS	SUGARS	FIBRE	PROTEIN	SALT
279	3.0g	1.0g	13.0g	3.0g	6.0g	47.0g	0.90g

Grocery Store Grab & Go

The secret to most successful cooks' home cooking comes from knowing when to cheat! With quality ingredients that come pre-prepped, pre-made or as powerhouses of flavour packed into jars, you can simplify your time spent in the kitchen without skimping on quality. Time to look at your grocery store in a whole new light!

Herbed Crispy Mushroom & Feta Bowl

Serves:
2

Equipment:
Large frying pan

Cook's Notes:
The key to creating a deep crisp on the mushrooms is to resist the temptation to move them too much: this just releases the moisture and makes them soggy.

2 tbsp olive oil

300g (10oz) mixed mushrooms, sliced

2 garlic cloves, thinly sliced

3 sprigs of thyme

20g (¾oz) unsalted butter

250g (9oz) packet mixed cooked grains

100g (3½oz) feta cheese, crumbled

3 tbsp chopped dill

handful of chopped flat-leaf parsley

good squeeze of lemon juice

2 tbsp extra-virgin olive oil

1. Heat the olive oil in a frying pan and add the mushrooms in a single layer. Cook over a medium–high heat, without moving, until they are golden and crisp. Turn over and cook for 1–2 minutes to crisp the other side, then add the garlic, thyme and butter. Season well with salt and pepper, then spoon the nutty butter over the mushrooms to coat.

2. Heat the grains according to the packet instruction and tip into a bowl. Toss with the feta, herbs, lemon juice and extra-virgin olive oil and season well. Serve with the crispy mushrooms.

COOK'S TIP

Keep it veggie: check the packaging on the feta to make sure it is vegetarian.

KCALS	FAT	SAT FAT	CARBS	SUGARS	FIBRE	PROTEIN	SALT
328	23.0g	8.0g	19.0g	1.0g	3.0g	9.0g	0.67g

Quinoa Veggie Salad

with Tahini Ranch Dressing

 (2) (VG)

Serves:
4, as a light
lunch

Equipment:
Saucepan

Cook's Notes:
A fantastic vegan dressing that ties together this crunchy,
crisp salad with lovely creaminess.

1 x 250g (9oz) packet
cooked quinoa

150g (5oz) radishes,
finely chopped

100g (3½oz) sugar snap peas,
finely chopped

150g (5oz) cooked
edamame beans

½ cucumber, peeled,
deseeded and chopped

2 cooked baby beetroot,
finely chopped

small handful of chopped dill

1 tbsp tahini

juice of 1 lemon

1 tbsp maple syrup

2 tbsp extra-virgin olive oil

1. Heat the grains in a saucepan with a splash of water, or
according to the packet instructions, and tip into a bowl.
Add all the vegetables and the dill and toss to combine.

2. Use a fork to blend the tahini with the lemon juice, maple
syrup and oil. Season with salt and pepper, drizzle over the
salad and serve.

KCALS	FAT	SAT FAT	CARBS	SUGARS	FIBRE	PROTEIN	SALT
278	12.0g	1.0g	27.0g	9.0g	7.0g	11.0g	0.19g

Teriyaki Tofu Bowl

with Cauliflower, Cucumber & Carrot

Serves:
2

Equipment:
Frying pan or
wok with lid

Cook's Notes:
If you have a bit of extra time you can press the tofu for up
to 30 minutes to extract even more water, then marinate
it for 15–20 minutes in a little extra teriyaki sauce before
cooking. You will find the tofu goes crispier and is even
more delicious.

250g (9oz) firm tofu

1 tbsp cornflour

3 tbsp sunflower oil

2 garlic cloves, crushed

2cm (¾in) piece of ginger,
peeled and grated

200g (7oz) ready-made
cauliflower rice (defrosted
if frozen)

4 tbsp teriyaki sauce

½ cucumber, peeled, deseeded
and julienned

2 carrots, peeled and julienned

1. Press the tofu firmly between kitchen paper to remove as
   much water as possible. Cut into 2cm (¾in) cubes and coat
   in the cornflour seasoned with salt and pepper.

2. Heat half the oil in a frying pan or wok and fry the tofu over
   a high heat until golden all over – allow a crust to form on all
   sides. Remove from the pan and set aside.

3. Add the remaining oil to the pan and fry the garlic and ginger
   for 1–2 minutes, then add the cauliflower rice and a splash
   of water, cover and steam for 2–3 minutes. Remove from the
   pan and set aside.

4. Add the tofu back to the pan with the teriyaki sauce and
   return to the heat to bubble until the tofu is coated all over.

5. Serve the tofu on a bed of cauliflower rice with the cucumber
   and carrots arranged around the bowl. Serve immediately.

KCALS	FAT	SAT FAT	CARBS	SUGARS	FIBRE	PROTEIN	SALT
447	26.0g	2.0g	34.0g	24.0g	7.0g	16.0g	2.33g

Quick-fix Veggie Curry

(2) (V)

Serves:
4

Equipment:
Sauté pan

Cook's Notes:
A good-quality shop-bought curry paste is a fantastic time-saver in the kitchen.

2 tbsp sunflower oil

3 tbsp rogan josh paste

2 x 225g (8oz) blocks paneer, cubed

1 x 400g (14oz) tin chickpeas, drained and rinsed

1 tbsp garam masala

150g (5oz) kale, tough stems removed and leaves finely shredded

250g (7oz) baby spinach

100g (3½oz) full-fat natural yoghurt

250g (9oz) pack cooked basmati rice

1. Heat the oil in a sauté pan over a medium–high heat and fry the curry paste for 1 minute, then add the paneer, increase the heat to high and fry for 1–2 minutes until lightly browned.

2. Add 200ml (¾ cup) water, the chickpeas and garam masala and allow to bubble for 5 minutes, then stir in the kale, spinach and yoghurt and bubble for about 1 minute more until the greens have wilted.

3. Steam the rice according to the packet instructions and serve with the curry.

KCALS	FAT	SAT FAT	CARBS	SUGARS	FIBRE	PROTEIN	SALT
667	40.0g	19.0g	33.0g	4.0g	6.0g	40.0g	0.65g

One-pan Fried Rice

(1) (V)

Serves:
4

Equipment:
Wok or frying
pan with lid

Cook's Notes:
Fried rice is the equivalent of Chinese comfort food –
warm and nourishing, and best eaten curled up on the
sofa in front of a good movie.

250g (9oz) pack cooked
basmati rice

2 tbsp sunflower oil

5cm (2in) piece of ginger,
peeled and grated

1 red chilli, finely chopped

6 spring onions, thinly sliced

300g (10oz) soya mince

1 tsp Chinese five spice

200g (7oz) bag shredded kale

150g (5oz) baby spinach

2 tbsp reduced salt soy sauce,
plus extra to serve

2 free-range eggs, beaten

handful of coriander leaves,
roughly chopped

1. Steam the rice in a microwave for 2 minutes, then tip into
   a bowl and allow to cool.

2. Meanwhile, heat half the oil in a wok or frying pan. Add
   the ginger, chilli and all but a handful of the spring onions
   and fry for 2–3 minutes. Add the soya mince and Chinese
   five spice, increase the heat and fry until browned all over.
   Add the kale, spinach and soy sauce and a splash of water,
   cover and cook for 2–3 minutes until the greens are tender.
   Tip into a bowl.

3. Add the rest of the oil to the wok or pan and heat over a
   medium–high heat. Add the beaten egg and swirl to coat
   the base of the pan thinly, like a pancake – allow to cook for
   1 minute until just set, then add the cooled rice and beat
   with a fork to combine and break up the egg 'pancake'.

4. Return the greens to the wok, add the coriander leaves
   and toss together. Serve scattered with the reserved spring
   onions and more soy sauce to taste.

KCALS	FAT	SAT FAT	CARBS	SUGARS	FIBRE	PROTEIN	SALT
295	10.0g	2.0g	31.0g	4.0g	4.0g	19.0g	1.31g

Spiced Prawns with Mexican Bean Stew & Avocado Salsa

Serves:	Equipment:	Cook's Notes:
4	Deep frying pan	Prawns are great at soaking up all the spicy flavour of this zingy Mexican stew.

2 tbsp olive oil

2 garlic cloves, crushed

1–2 tbsp chipotle paste

2 x 400g (14oz) tins mixed beans, drained and rinsed

1 x 400g (14oz) tin chopped tomatoes

2 x 150g (5oz) packets raw prawns

2 avocados, diced

1 small red onion, finely diced

juice of 1 lime

2 tbsp extra-virgin olive oil

large handful of chopped coriander

1. Heat the olive oil in a frying pan over a medium heat and gently fry the garlic and chipotle paste for 1 minute, then add the beans, the tomatoes and 100ml (½ cup) water. Season well with salt and pepper and bubble for 15 minutes until thickened and no longer raw-tasting.

2. Add the prawns and cook for 1–2 minutes until they are pink all over.

3. Meanwhile, mix the avocados with the onion and lime juice. Season well, drizzle over the extra-virgin olive oil and stir in half the coriander.

4. Scatter the rest of the coriander over the bean and prawn stew and serve with the avocado salsa.

KCALS	FAT	SAT FAT	CARBS	SUGARS	FIBRE	PROTEIN	SALT
431	27.0g	5.0g	19.0g	6.0g	10.0g	23.0g	1.04g

Hot Smoked Salmon & Chickpea Salad

with Shaved Fennel

Serves:
2

Equipment:
Salad bowl

Cook's Notes:
This would also work brilliantly with smoked mackerel or a pot of white crabmeat, so see what you can grab on your way home.

150g (5oz) hot smoked salmon

1 x 400g (14oz) tin chickpeas, drained and rinsed

1 fennel bulb, very thinly sliced

1 lemon

70g (2½oz) bag wild rocket

150g (5oz) low-fat Greek yoghurt

2 tsp capers, drained, rinsed and roughly chopped

2 tbsp chopped dill, plus extra to garnish

2 tbsp extra-virgin olive oil

1. Flake the salmon into a bowl and toss with the chickpeas and fennel.

2. Using a sharp knife, remove the rind and white pith from the lemon and segment the pieces (do this over a bowl to catch the juice). Cut each segment in half and add them to the salad bowl with the rocket.

3. Squeeze the remaining juice from the lemon skin into the bowl of juice and add the yoghurt, capers and dill. Season well.

4. Drizzle the salad with the oil and a good sprinkle of sea salt and cracked black pepper, then serve with the yoghurt and extra dill to garnish.

KCALS	FAT	SAT FAT	CARBS	SUGARS	FIBRE	PROTEIN	SALT
490	22.0g	3.0g	29.0g	5.0g	12.0g	39.0g	2.07g

One-pan Tomato & Bean Fish Chowder

Serves:
4

Equipment:
Deep saucepan

Cook's Notes:
Soffritto, also called a mirepoix, is a classic base of finely chopped onion, carrot and celery that is the starting point of so many recipes. These days, you don't need superb knife skills as you can buy it pre-chopped from the supermarket.

1 tbsp olive oil

500g (1lb 2oz) soffritto mix or vegetable soup mix

1 x 600ml jar (2½ cups) passata

500ml (2 cups) vegetable stock

4 x 150g (5oz) haddock fillets

1 x 400g (14oz) tin cannellini beans, drained and rinsed

large handful of basil leaves

1. Heat the oil in a deep saucepan and gently fry the soffritto or vegetable mix for 5 minutes over a medium heat until softened. Add the passata and vegetable stock to the pan and bring to a steady simmer.

2. Add the haddock and beans, cover and simmer for 4–5 minutes until the fish is cooked through and starting to break into chunks. Scatter with basil leaves and serve.

KCALS	FAT	SAT FAT	CARBS	SUGARS	FIBRE	PROTEIN	SALT
286	5.0g	1.0g	24.0g	14.0g	9.0g	32.0g	0.89g

Za'atar Spiced Tuna & Lentil Salad

Serves:
4

Equipment:
Saucepan

Cook's Notes:
Za'atar is a fragrant Lebanese spice blend full of thyme, oregano and sesame seeds.

1 x 250g (9oz) tub hummus

finely grated zest of ½ lemon, plus a squeeze of juice

2 tsp za'atar

1 x 250g (9oz) pack pre-cooked Puy lentils

2 tsp red wine vinegar

2–3 tbsp extra-virgin olive oil

2 avocados, sliced

1 cucumber, peeled, deseeded and cut into half-moons

2 x 220g (8oz) jars top-quality tuna in olive oil, drained

handful of flat-leaf parsley, chopped

1. Mix the hummus with the lemon zest and za'atar and set aside.

2. Warm the lentils in a saucepan with a dash of water, or according to the packet instructions, and tip into a bowl. Add the vinegar, lemon juice and oil and season well with salt and pepper.

3. Take four bowls and spread a splodge of hummus in the base of each one. Top with the lentils and arrange the avocado slices, cucumber and tuna around the bowls. Scatter each bowl with parsley and serve.

KCALS	FAT	SAT FAT	CARBS	SUGARS	FIBRE	PROTEIN	SALT
657	45.0g	5.0g	27.0g	2.0g	10.0g	31.0g	1.62g

Thai-style Rotisserie Chicken Salad

Serves:
4

Equipment:
Salad bowl

Cook's Notes:
Not all rotisserie chickens were created equal, and many are not responsibly farmed. Look out for those birds that are free-range and hormone-free, from suppliers who pay attention to animal welfare standards. If you can't find one, try slow-roasting your own free-range organic chicken at the weekend to use for easy midweek suppers like this one.

1 rotisserie chicken, meat removed and shredded (about 600g/1lb 5oz)

2 carrots, peeled and julienned

1 cucumber, peeled, deseeded and diced

¼ red cabbage, shredded

juice of 1–2 limes

1 tbsp reduced salt soy sauce

3 tbsp fish sauce

3 tbsp peanut butter

large handful of coriander, roughly chopped

3 spring onions, thinly sliced

1. Add the chicken, carrots, cucumber and cabbage to a bowl.

2. Mix the lime juice with the soy sauce, fish sauce and peanut butter, pour over the salad and toss together.

3. Serve scattered with the coriander and spring onions.

KCALS	FAT	SAT FAT	CARBS	SUGARS	FIBRE	PROTEIN	SALT
372	18.0g	5.0g	9.0g	7.0g	5.0G	40.0g	4.50g

Hoisin Chicken Stir-fry
with Pak Choi & Celery

Serves:	Equipment:	Cook's Notes:
4	Wok or frying pan	Celery adds a pleasing green freshness as well as loads of protective antioxidants to this sticky chicken stir-fry.

1 tbsp sunflower oil

4 skinless chicken breasts, diced

2cm (¾in) piece of ginger, peeled and grated

6 celery sticks, halved lengthways and then sliced

4 tbsp hoisin sauce

2 tbsp tomato ketchup

1 tbsp reduced salt soy sauce

1 tsp Chinese five spice

2 pak choi, quartered

1. Heat the oil in a wok or frying pan. Add the chicken, ginger and celery, and fry over a high heat for 4–5 minutes.

2. Add the hoisin sauce, ketchup, soy sauce and Chinese five spice and cook, stirring, for 3–4 minutes.

3. Add the pak choi and a splash of water and cook for 1–2 minutes more, then serve.

KCALS	FAT	SAT FAT	CARBS	SUGARS	FIBRE	PROTEIN	SALT
325	10.0g	0.3g	10.0g	7.0g	2.0g	48.0g	1.54g

Kung Po Chicken Salad

(2)

Serves:
4

Equipment:
Large frying pan

Cook's Notes:
This veggie-loaded salad stretches a smaller amount of chicken to more people. If you want to pep it up, try adding a finely chopped red chilli when you cook the chicken.

1 tbsp olive oil

2 skinless chicken breasts, butterflied

1½ tsp Chinese five spice

1 romaine lettuce, shredded

1 x 400g (14oz) bag mixed prepared vegetables (eg carrots, red pepper, sugar snaps, green beans, baby corn)

2 tbsp sweet chilli sauce

1 tbsp rice vinegar

3 tbsp reduced salt soy sauce

1 tbsp toasted sesame seeds

4 spring onions, thinly sliced

1. Heat the oil in a large frying pan. Season the chicken with salt and pepper and a sprinkle of the Chinese five spice and fry for 3–4 minutes on each side until golden and cooked through. Set aside to rest and cool a little, then slice or shred.

2. Toss the chicken with the lettuce and mixed veg in a bowl.

3. Use a fork to blend the sweet chilli sauce with the remaining Chinese five spice, the rice vinegar and soy sauce, then pour over the salad and toss well. Scatter with the sesame seeds and spring onions and serve.

KCALS	FAT	SAT FAT	CARBS	SUGARS	FIBRE	PROTEIN	SALT
246	8.0g	1.0g	12.0g	10.0g	7.0g	28.0g	1.52g

Harissa Chicken

with Rainbow Salad

Serves:
4

Equipment:
Sauté pan

Cook's Notes:
You can get lots of different kinds of harissa paste, but the rose variety has an extra layer of deliciousness – do keep an eye out for it.

1 tbsp olive oil

6 boneless, skinless chicken thighs

3 tbsp rose harissa paste

finely grated zest and juice of ½ lemon

2 tbsp low-fat Greek yoghurt

3 tbsp extra-virgin olive oil

1 x 220g (8oz) bag rainbow salad

1 avocado, sliced

1 x 400g (14oz) tin chickpeas, drained and rinsed

handful of chopped flat-leaf parsley

1. Heat the olive oil in a sauté pan. Season the chicken with salt and pepper and spread all over with the harissa paste and a sprinkling of lemon zest. Fry over a medium–high heat for 3–4 minutes on each side until just cooked through. Set aside to rest, then slice and combine with the yoghurt while the chicken is still warm.

2. Mix the lemon juice with some seasoning in a salad bowl and whisk in the extra-virgin olive oil.

3. Add the rainbow salad, avocado, chickpeas and parsley and toss gently to combine. Serve with the harissa chicken.

KCALS	FAT	SAT FAT	CARBS	SUGARS	FIBRE	PROTEIN	SALT
433	28.0g	5.0g	14.0g	2.0g	7.0g	27.0g	0.65g

Rotisserie Chicken Plate

with Lemon Harissa & Herb Tossed Lettuces

Serves:
4

Equipment:
Saucepan,
small frying pan

Cook's Notes:
This is an ideal recipe to use up any leftover vegetables, so raid the fridge and add plenty of colourful salad veg. Serve with warm flatbreads and a scattering of pomegranate seeds, and you have an instant midweek dinner party dish.

200g (7oz) mixed
lettuce leaves

1 rotisserie chicken,
meat removed and shredded
(about 600g/1lb 5oz)

1 tbsp wholegrain mustard

2 tsp cumin seeds, toasted

1 tbsp extra-virgin olive oil

large handful of
coriander leaves

large handful of young
flat-leaf parsley leaves

For the lemon harissa

3 tbsp rose harissa paste

2 garlic cloves, crushed

finely grated zest and
juice of 1 lemon

3–4 tbsp extra-virgin olive oil

1. Put the lettuce leaves into a salad bowl with the chicken meat.

2. Mix the mustard, cumin seeds, oil and some seasoning together and pour over the leaves and chicken. Add the herbs and toss together.

3. To make the dressing, whisk the harissa paste, garlic, lemon zest and juice together with some seasoning, then whisk in the oil.

4. Divide the chicken and salad between plates and serve with the lemon harissa to drizzle over the top.

KCALS	FAT	SAT FAT	CARBS	SUGARS	FIBRE	PROTEIN	SALT
419	28.0g	5.0g	4.0g	2.0g	3.0g	36.0g	1.72g

Pesto Sausage Pizza

① 🌿

Serves:
4

Equipment:
Frying pan,
2 baking sheets

Cook's Notes:
Pizzas are so versatile: it's a great idea to keep a stash
of pizza bases in your freezer so you can always throw
together a speedy supper with a few grabbed ingredients.

6 herby sausages

1 tbsp olive oil

4 individual pizza bases

75g (2½oz) fresh basil pesto

2 x 125g (4oz) buffalo
mozzarella balls, torn

120g (4oz) cherry tomatoes,
halved

200g (7oz) ready-made
pickled cabbage (sauerkraut)

1. Preheat the oven to as hot as it will go.

2. Squeeze the meat from the sausage casings. Heat the oil
   in a frying pan over a high heat and brown the sausage
   meat, breaking it up with a spoon, until golden and
   cooked through.

3. Put the pizza bases onto baking sheets. Divide the sausage
   meat between them, drizzle 1 tablespoon of the pesto on
   each base and scatter with the mozzarella and tomatoes.

4. Bake for 10 minutes until the bases are crisp and golden
   and the cheese is melting. Drizzle with the rest of the pesto
   and serve with the pickled cabbage.

KCALS	FAT	SAT FAT	CARBS	SUGARS	FIBRE	PROTEIN	SALT
829	38.0g	13.0g	87.0g	7.0g	7.0g	30.0g	3.97g

Spicy & Sticky Marmalade Pork

(2)

Serves:	**Equipment:**	**Cook's Notes:**
2	Sauté pan or frying pan with lid	Marmalade is such a great ingredient: it really boosts this most simple of dishes with its tangy, deep, sweet and citrus flavour.

1 tbsp olive oil

1 red onion, thinly sliced

1 garlic clove, crushed

good pinch of chilli flakes

1 x 350g (12oz) packet stir-fry pork strips

5 tbsp orange and ginger marmalade

200g (7oz) shredded greens, such as spring greens or baby kale

1. Heat the oil in a frying pan over a medium heat and gently fry the onion, garlic and chilli flakes for 5 minutes until soft.

2. Move the onion to the side of the pan and increase the heat. Add the pork strips and fry until browned all over – keep stirring the onion to prevent it catching. Add the marmalade and 80–100ml (scant ½ cup) water and stir to create a sauce; bring to a steady simmer.

3. Add the greens, cover and cook for 2–3 minutes until the greens are wilted and the pork is tender and sticky.

KCALS	FAT	SAT FAT	CARBS	SUGARS	FIBRE	PROTEIN	SALT
436	14.0g	2.0g	33.0g	29.0g	7.0g	42.0g	0.34g

Harissa Lamb & Lentil Salad with Whipped Feta

①

Serves:
4

Equipment:
Frying pan

Cook's Notes:
If you want you can make this a veggie dish by roasting wedges of butternut squash in place of the lamb.

400g (14oz) lamb mince

1 tsp cumin seeds

1 tbsp harissa paste

2 tbsp chopped flat-leaf parsley

2 tsp olive oil

½ x 200g (7oz) bag sliced kale

2 tbsp extra-virgin olive oil

2 x 250g (9oz) packet cooked Puy lentils

squeeze of lemon juice

150g (5oz) feta cheese, crumbled

150g (5oz) low-fat Greek yoghurt

1. In a bowl, mix the lamb mince with the cumin seeds and 2 teaspoons of the harissa paste and the parsley. Season well and shape into 12 small patties.

2. Heat the olive oil in a frying pan and fry the patties for 2–3 minutes on each side until golden and cooked through.

3. Meanwhile massage the kale with half the extra-virgin olive oil to soften it. Season with salt and pepper and tip into a bowl. Warm the lentils according to the packet instructions and add to the kale along with the rest of the extra-virgin olive oil, a squeeze of lemon juice and some seasoning.

4. Whip the feta and yoghurt together with a fork or whisk until creamy. Swirl through the rest of the harissa and season with plenty of black pepper. Serve the lamb patties with the lentils and a dollop of the whipped feta.

KCALS	FAT	SAT FAT	CARBS	SUGARS	FIBRE	PROTEIN	SALT
586	31.0g	13.0g	30.0g	4.0g	8.0g	43.0g	1.29g

Crunchy Thai Beef & Mango Salad

(4)

Serves:	Equipment:	Cook's Notes:
2	Griddle pan or sauté pan	A really colourful and zingy recipe to brighten up a midweek dinner.

1 tsp sunflower oil

225g (8oz) sirloin steak, trimmed of excess fat

3 tbsp sweet chilli sauce

juice of 1 lime

1 cucumber, peeled, deseeded and shaved into ribbons

2 carrots, peeled and shaved into ribbons

1 x 280g (9¾oz) packet ready-diced mango (cut larger pieces into smaller dice)

2 baby gem lettuces, leaves separated

handful of coriander leaves

2–3 sprigs of mint, leaves picked

1. Heat the oil in a griddle or sauté pan until smoking hot and sear the steak for 1–2 minutes on each side until browned but still rare in the middle. Set aside to rest.

2. Mix the sweet chilli sauce with the lime juice in a serving bowl. Add the cucumber, carrots, mango and baby gem lettuces, along with the herbs, and toss through to combine.

3. Slice the steak and serve on top of the salad.

KCALS	FAT	SAT FAT	CARBS	SUGARS	FIBRE	PROTEIN	SALT
435	15.0g	6.0g	39.0g	39.0g	10.0g	30.0g	1.02g

Pan-fried Steak & Veggie Tacos

Serves:
4

Equipment:
2 frying pans

Cook's Notes:
Try these tacos – they make cooking for friends midweek a breeze.

2 sirloin steaks

2 tbsp olive oil

1 tbsp Cajun or fajita seasoning

500g (1lb 2oz) packet pre-sliced mixed peppers

200g (7oz) low-fat Greek yoghurt

1 garlic clove, crushed

large handful of coriander leaves

4 flour tortillas

1 avocado, sliced

hot sauce, to serve

1. Place a frying pan over a medium–high heat while you rub the steaks with 1 tablespoon of the oil and season with the Cajun or fajita mix. Add to the hot pan and fry for 2 minutes on each side until charred but still blushing pink in the middle. Remove from the pan and set aside to rest.

2. Let the pan cool a little, then add the rest of the oil and the peppers and fry them for a few minutes until soft.

3. Meanwhile, mix the yoghurt and garlic together. Chop all but a few of the coriander leaves and mix into the yoghurt.

4. Warm the tortillas in a dry frying pan while you slice the steak into strips. Serve the tortillas with a splodge of yoghurt, some fried peppers, steak strips and avocado. Drizzle with hot sauce, scatter with a few coriander leaves, wrap and serve.

KCALS	FAT	SAT FAT	CARBS	SUGARS	FIBRE	PROTEIN	SALT
417	22.0g	7.0g	30.0g	9.0g	6.0g	23.0g	1.00g

15-minute Meals

Fast flavour is found in good-quality ingredients and simple cooking methods with minimal prep. This collection of dinners is designed to bring simple meals to the table in 15 minutes or less.

Kale Cacio e Pepe

Serves:
2

Equipment:
Wide shallow pan, large high-sided frying pan

Cook's Notes:
Despite the incredible simplicity of its ingredients, a true cacio e pepe takes a little practice in order to get right the almost alchemical blend of cheese and water to form that glossy, coating sauce. Though as it is so delicious, you won't mind how many times you practise making it!

200g (7oz) dried spaghetti

150g (5oz) kale, tough stems removed and leaves finely shredded

20g (¾oz) unsalted butter

2 tsp black peppercorns, crushed

80g (3oz) pecorino cheese, grated

1. Bring a shallow pan of water to the boil with plenty of salt. Add the pasta (the water should only just cover it) and simmer for 10–12 minutes until the pasta is tender, adding the kale 3–4 minutes before the end of the pasta cooking time.

2. At the same time, melt the butter in a large, high-sided frying pan, add the black peppercorns, then tip into a large bowl. Add the pecorino and mix together. Scoop out 250ml (1 cup) of the pasta water while the pasta is still cooking and beat a little splash into the bowl to make a paste, then keep adding water gradually until you have a smooth sauce.

3. Drain the pasta and add it to the bowl of cheesy sauce along with the kale. Stir together, adding a little more pasta water until the whole thing is coated in a glorious glossy sauce. Serve immediately.

COOK'S TIP

Make it veggie: swap the pecorino for a vegetarian alternative.

KCALS	FAT	SAT FAT	CARBS	SUGARS	FIBRE	PROTEIN	SALT
627	23.0g	13.0g	75.0g	3.0g	8.0g	25.0g	2.09g

Super Green Pesto Pasta

🌿
①

Serves:	Equipment:	Cook's Notes:
6	Food processor, frying pan, saucepan	You won't regret making your own pesto over the shop-bought variety. It has so much more flavour and vibrancy that you may never buy it again.

50g (2oz) basil leaves

30g (1oz) Parmesan cheese, grated, plus extra to serve

50g (2oz) pine nuts, plus extra to serve

1 large garlic clove

85ml (⅓ cup) extra-virgin olive oil, plus extra for frying

2 courgettes, diced

300g (10oz) frozen peas

500g (1lb 2oz) fresh tagliatelle

1. In a food processor blitz the basil with the Parmesan, pine nuts and garlic, season well with salt and pepper and gradually whizz in the oil until you have a glossy pesto.

2. Heat a little oil in a frying pan and fry the courgettes for 2–3 minutes until lightly coloured. Add the frozen peas and allow to defrost and warm through.

3. Cook the pasta in a saucepan of boiling salted water for 2–3 minutes, then drain and add to the pan of veg along with the pesto. Serve with a scattering of pine nuts and Parmesan.

COOK'S TIP

Make it veggie: swap the Parmesan for a vegetarian alternative.

KCALS	FAT	SAT FAT	CARBS	SUGARS	FIBRE	PROTEIN	SALT
498	24.0g	4.0g	52.0g	4.0g	3.0g	16.0g	0.15g

Cauliflower & Artichoke Vodka Pasta

(3)

Serves:
4

Equipment:
Saucepan,
box grater,
large frying pan

Cook's Notes:
The cream and Parmesan in this dish may make you think it's rather indulgent, but both artichokes and cauliflower are loaded with nutrients to give this dish a boost of health-giving benefits.

300g (10oz) dried rigatoni

250g (9oz) cauliflower

3 tbsp olive oil

1 large onion, finely chopped

2 garlic cloves, crushed

3 tbsp tomato purée

280g (9¾oz) jarred artichokes, drained and chopped

80ml (⅓ cup) vodka

200ml (¾ cup) single cream

50g (2oz) Parmesan cheese, grated

1. Cook the pasta in a saucepan of boiling salted water for 12 minutes. Drain, reserving a cup of the cooking water.

2. At the same time, coarsely grate the cauliflower. Heat the oil in a large frying pan and gently fry the onion over a medium heat for 5 minutes until softened. Add the garlic and grated cauliflower, increase the heat and fry for 1–2 minutes until lightly browned, then add the tomato purée, artichokes and vodka. Bubble away for 1 minute, then add the reserved pasta water and cream and season well with salt and pepper. Cook for 2 minutes.

3. Add the pasta and toss to coat all over, then serve with the Parmesan and lots of cracked black pepper.

COOK'S TIP

Make it veggie: swap the Parmesan for a vegetarian alternative.

KCALS	FAT	SAT FAT	CARBS	SUGARS	FIBRE	PROTEIN	SALT
605	26.0g	10.0g	59.0g	9.0g	9.0g	18.0g	1.80g

Tomato & Feta Salad Flatbreads

 (1) (V)

Serves:
4

Equipment:
Frying pan

Cook's Notes:
When the tomato season is high, look out for heirloom tomatoes in an array of sizes and colours – they look fabulous and taste great.

250g (9oz) heirloom tomatoes, sliced or quartered (depending on size)

3 tbsp extra-virgin olive oil

1 garlic clove, crushed

1 tsp ground cumin

1 tsp ground coriander

good pinch of sumac or chilli flakes

handful of chopped flat-leaf parsley

4 flatbreads

4 dollops of low-fat Greek yoghurt

¼ cucumber, peeled, deseeded and grated

150g (5oz) feta cheese, crumbled

1. Put the tomatoes into a bowl with 2 tablespoons of the oil, the garlic, spices and half the parsley. Season well with salt and pepper and set aside.

2. Warm the flatbreads in a dry frying pan.

3. Mix the yoghurt with the rest of the parsley and the cucumber and season well.

4. Splodge the yoghurt onto the flatbreads, top with the marinated tomatoes and scatter with the feta. Drizzle with the last of the oil and a good grinding of black pepper and serve.

> COOK'S TIP
>
> Keep it veggie: check the packaging on the feta to make sure it is vegetarian.

KCALS	FAT	SAT FAT	CARBS	SUGARS	FIBRE	PROTEIN	SALT
405	18.0g	7.0g	43.0g	7.0g	4.0g	15.0g	1.13g

Cauliflower Rice Tabbouleh

with Sun-blushed Tomatoes & Fried Halloumi

Serves:
4

Equipment:
Non-stick
frying pan

Cook's Notes:
Keeping the cauliflower raw gives a satisfying bite to
this super-simple dish.

700g (1½lb) riced cauliflower
*(shop-bought or see Cook's
Notes on page 124)*

large bunch of flat-leaf parsley,
finely chopped

handful of mint leaves,
finely chopped

5 spring onions, thinly sliced

150g (5oz) sun-blushed
tomatoes

½ cucumber, peeled,
deseeded and finely diced

finely grated zest and juice
of 1 lemon

3 tbsp extra-virgin olive oil

250g (9oz) halloumi cheese,
thickly sliced

1 tbsp balsamic vinegar

2 tsp clear honey

1. In a large bowl toss the cauliflower rice with the herbs,
   spring onions, tomatoes and cucumber. Add the lemon
   zest and juice, oil and plenty of seasoning.

2. Place a non-stick frying pan over a medium heat. Fry the
   halloumi slices for 1–2 minutes each side until golden brown.
   Add the vinegar and honey to the pan and allow it to coat
   the cheese and become sticky. Serve straight away with
   the tabbouleh.

KCALS	FAT	SAT FAT	CARBS	SUGARS	FIBRE	PROTEIN	SALT
431	27.0g	12.0g	21.0g	15.0g	9.0g	22.0g	2.79g

Green Miso Spaghetti

(1) (V)

Serves:	Equipment:	Cook's Notes:
4	Saucepan, frying pan, small saucepan	Incredibly moreish, this dish has bags of umami to tickle your taste buds.

350g (12oz) dried spaghetti

2 tbsp olive oil

3 banana shallots, finely chopped

250g (9oz) spring greens, shredded

100g (3½oz) unsalted butter

3 tbsp red miso paste

1. Cook the pasta in a saucepan of boiling salted water for 10–12 minutes, then drain, reserving a cup of the cooking water.

2. Meanwhile, heat the oil in a frying pan and fry the shallots for 5 minutes until soft but not coloured. Add the greens and a splash of the pasta water, cover and cook for 2–3 minutes.

3. Melt the butter with the miso paste and blend with 150ml (2/3 cup) of the pasta water until smooth. Add to the drained pasta with the greens. Serve with lots of cracked black pepper.

KCALS	FAT	SAT FAT	CARBS	SUGARS	FIBRE	PROTEIN	SALT
604	29.0g	14.0g	69.0g	5.0g	7.0g	14.0g	1.33g

Spicy Tofu & Mushroom Stir-fry

(2) (VG)

Serves:
2

Equipment:
Wok or
frying pan

Cook's Notes:
To get the tofu to take on colour you need to make sure it is as dry as possible. Start with a block of extra-firm tofu – if you can find it – and then press it firmly between sheets of kitchen paper several times to remove as much moisture as you can.

280g (9¾oz) firm tofu

3 tbsp sunflower oil

170g (6oz) mixed Asian mushrooms (shiitake, oyster, enoki), torn into equal-sized pieces

4 spring onions, cut into 2cm (¾in) pieces

150g (5oz) sugar snap peas

2cm (¾in) piece of ginger, peeled and grated

1 red chilli, deseeded and finely chopped

3 tbsp reduced salt soy sauce

2 tbsp rice vinegar

1 tbsp chilli bean sauce

handful of coriander leaves, chopped

1. Press the tofu firmly between sheets of kitchen paper to dry it out, then cut into 2cm (¾in) cubes. Heat 1 tablespoon of the oil in a wok or frying pan and fry the tofu cubes for a few minutes, turning, until golden brown. Remove to a plate, add another tablespoon of oil to the pan and fry the mushrooms over a high heat until they are browned all over. Add to the tofu.

2. Heat the remaining tablespoon of oil in the pan and add the spring onions, sugar snap peas, ginger and chilli and fry for a few minutes over a medium heat to soften. Mix in the soy sauce, rice vinegar and chilli bean sauce and cook for 1 minute, then return the mushrooms and tofu to the pan and toss well until everything is combined.

3. Serve with a scattering of coriander leaves.

KCALS	FAT	SAT FAT	CARBS	SUGARS	FIBRE	PROTEIN	SALT
454	29.0g	3.0g	15.0g	8.0g	6.0g	29.0g	3.20g

Satay Noodle Stir-fry

(2) (VG)

Serves:	**Equipment:**	**Cook's Notes:**
4	Wok or frying pan	Full of crunch and freshness, this light vegan dish is great for lunch or a late-night dinner.

1 tbsp sunflower oil

2 garlic cloves, thinly sliced

2cm (¾in) piece of ginger, peeled and grated

320g (11¼oz) tenderstem broccoli, stems halved

250g (9oz) sugar snap peas

300g (10oz) straight-to-wok udon noodles

4 spring onions, thinly sliced

For the sauce

5 tbsp peanut butter

1 tbsp reduced salt soy sauce

1 tbsp rice vinegar

2 tbsp sesame oil

1. Use a fork to blend all the ingredients for the sauce together with 2–3 tablespoons water.

2. Heat the oil in a wok or frying pan over a high heat, add the garlic and ginger and cook for 1 minute. Add the broccoli and sugar snap peas and a splash of water and cook for 2–3 minutes until just tender, then add the noodles and fry for 1 minute more.

3. Add the sauce and bubble for 1 minute until the vegetables are all coated and the sauce is slightly thickened. Serve with a scattering of spring onions.

KCALS	FAT	SAT FAT	CARBS	SUGARS	FIBRE	PROTEIN	SALT
355	19.0g	4.0g	28.0g	6.0g	8.0g	15.0g	0.84g

Scallops with Green Peas & Asparagus

Serves:
4

Equipment:
Saucepan,
frying pan

Cook's Notes:
Creamy, tender scallops and sweet peas and asparagus tied together with salty Parmesan and gloriously nutty brown butter.

350g (12oz) frozen peas

2–3 tbsp extra-virgin olive oil

2 sprigs of mint, leaves picked

1 tbsp olive oil

bunch of asparagus, trimmed

12 fat king scallops, with or without roe

25g (1oz) unsalted butter

20g (¾oz) grated Parmesan cheese

1. Cook the peas in a saucepan of boiling water for 2–3 minutes, then drain, reserving 100ml (½ cup) of the cooking water. Blitz two-thirds of the peas with half the extra-virgin olive oil, the reserved cooking water and almost all of the mint leaves. Season and set aside.

2. Heat half the olive oil in a frying pan and sear the asparagus until lightly charred and just cooked. Set aside with the unblitzed peas and keep warm.

3. Pat the scallops dry with kitchen paper. Add the butter to the hot pan and when it starts to bubble, add the scallops and sear them for 1–2 minutes on each side, spooning the brown butter over the top after you turn them.

4. Put a splodge of pea purée onto four plates, top with the charred asparagus and peas and the golden scallops. Drizzle with the remaining extra-virgin olive oil and scatter with Parmesan shavings and the reserved mint leaves.

KCALS	FAT	SAT FAT	CARBS	SUGARS	FIBRE	PROTEIN	SALT
279	19.0g	6.0g	11.0g	6.0g	6.0g	13.0g	0.54g

Spaghetti al Limone with Prawns & Broccolini

🍋 ①

Serves:
4

Equipment:
Saucepan,
frying pan

Cook's Notes:
Comfort food at its best – with fragrant lemon and sweet
juicy prawns.

350g (12oz) dried spaghetti

320g (11¼oz) tenderstem
broccoli

1 tbsp unsalted butter

1 garlic clove, thinly sliced

pinch of chilli flakes

finely grated zest of 1 lemon,
plus a squeeze of juice

100ml (½ cup) single cream

30g (1oz) grated
Parmesan cheese

150g (5oz) cooked prawns

1. Cook the pasta in a saucepan of boiling salted water for
   10 minutes, adding the broccoli to the pan for the last
   3–4 minutes of cooking. Just before the cooking time
   is up, remove 200ml (¾ cup) of the cooking water and
   set aside.

2. Meanwhile, melt the butter in a frying pan over a medium
   heat, add the garlic, chilli flakes and lemon zest and cook
   for 30 seconds until fragrant. Add the cream and Parmesan
   and whisk well to combine. Gradually whisk in enough
   of the pasta water to make a glossy sauce.

3. Drain the pasta and broccoli and add to the sauce with
   the prawns; toss to combine, adding more pasta water
   if needed. Check the seasoning, add a little squeeze of
   lemon juice and serve immediately.

KCALS	FAT	SAT FAT	CARBS	SUGARS	FIBRE	PROTEIN	SALT
494	12.0g	7.0g	69.0g	4.0g	7.0g	24.0g	0.80g

Crispy Salmon with Asparagus & Cherry Tomato Sauce

ⓐ①

Serves:
4

Equipment:
Deep sauté pan

Cook's Notes:
A super-food supper if ever there was one. Packed with omega-3 fatty acids, vitamins, minerals and lycopene from the tomatoes, an antioxidant that helps protect cell damage.

1 tbsp olive oil

4 skin-on salmon fillets

250g (9oz) asparagus, trimmed

2 garlic cloves, thinly sliced

150g (5oz) cherry tomatoes, halved

squeeze of lemon juice

handful of basil leaves

1. Heat the oil in a deep sauté pan. Add the salmon fillets, skin-side down, and the asparagus. Fry gently over a low–medium heat until the salmon is crispy and the asparagus is slightly charred.

2. Turn the fish over, add the garlic and cook for 1 minute, then add the cherry tomatoes and a little splash of water and cook for 4–5 minutes until the tomatoes have started to break down. Add plenty of seasoning and a squeeze of lemon juice. Scatter over the basil leaves and serve.

KCALS	FAT	SAT FAT	CARBS	SUGARS	FIBRE	PROTEIN	SALT
335	23.0g	4.0g	3.0g	2.0g	2.0g	29.0g	0.15g

One-pan Chicken Parmesan

Serves:
4

Equipment:
Ovenproof
frying pan

Cook's Notes:
A speedy twist on an Italian classic. You can find pre-prepared courgette spaghetti in many supermarkets or easily make it yourself with a julienne peeler.

2 tbsp olive oil

500g (1lb 2oz) mini chicken breast fillets

1 tsp each of dried oregano and dried thyme

300ml (1¼ cups) passata

350g (12oz) courgette spaghetti

100g (3½oz) mozzarella cheese, grated

75g (2½oz) Parmesan cheese, grated

75g (2½oz) panko breadcrumbs

handful of basil leaves

1. Preheat the grill to high. Heat the oil in an ovenproof frying pan and fry the chicken over a high heat until browned all over. Add the dried herbs and passata and season well with salt and pepper, then add the courgette spaghetti and warm through until a little softened.

2. Mix the cheeses with the breadcrumbs and scatter all over the top of the pan. Pop under the grill for 4–5 minutes until golden and bubbling.

3. Serve scattered with basil leaves.

KCALS	FAT	SAT FAT	CARBS	SUGARS	FIBRE	PROTEIN	SALT
451	21.0g	8.0g	20.0g	6.0g	3.0g	44.0g	1.02g

Pad See Ew

Serves:
4

Equipment:
Wok

Cook's Notes:
An immensely popular Thai street food dish that is super-simple to create at home in less than 15 minutes.

250g (9oz) wide rice noodles

2 tbsp oyster sauce

3 tbsp reduced salt soy sauce

2 tsp white wine vinegar

2 tsp caster sugar

1 tbsp sunflower oil

2 garlic cloves, crushed

4 skinless chicken thigh fillets, cut into 1cm (½in) dice

320g (11¼oz) tenderstem broccoli, stems cut into thirds

1 large free-range egg

1. Soak the noodles in boiling water for 10 minutes, or until softened. Whisk the oyster and soy sauces, vinegar and sugar together and set aside.

2. While the noodles are soaking, heat the oil in a wok over a high heat, add the garlic and fry for 30 seconds, then add the chicken and stir-fry for 2–3 minutes until nearly cooked. Add the broccoli and a splash of water and cook for 2–3 minutes more.

3. Push the chicken and broccoli to the side of the wok and crack in the egg; scramble until just set, then mix with the chicken and broccoli. Remove from the wok and set aside.

4. Drain the noodles and add to the wok with the sauce and toss together to coat and heat through. Return the chicken and broccoli to the pan and mix together, then serve immediately.

KCALS	FAT	SAT FAT	CARBS	SUGARS	FIBRE	PROTEIN	SALT
278	10.0g	2.0g	24.0g	4.0g	3.0g	20.0g	2.01g

Bacon & Egg Frisée Salad

①

Serves:	**Equipment:**	**Cook's Notes:**
4	Frying pan, slotted spoon	Otherwise known as Salade Lyonnaise, this warm salad looks fabulous as well as being really easy to make.

1 tbsp olive oil

200g (7oz) smoked bacon lardons

2 slices of sourdough bread, cut into 1cm (½in) cubes

150–200g (5–7oz) frisée lettuce, torn

2 tbsp white wine vinegar

1 tsp Dijon mustard

1 tbsp chopped tarragon

6 tbsp extra-virgin olive oil

4 large free-range eggs

2 tbsp chives, snipped

1. Heat the olive oil in a frying pan and fry the bacon for 2–3 minutes over a medium–high heat until crisp. Remove with a slotted spoon and set aside. Fry the bread in the bacon fat until crisp, then drain on kitchen paper.

2. Put the lettuce in a salad bowl and add the bacon and crispy bread.

3. Mix the vinegar with the mustard and tarragon and plenty of seasoning, then whisk in the extra-virgin olive oil to form a vinaigrette.

4. Bring a small saucepan of water to the boil, then reduce to a gentle simmer. One at a time, crack the eggs directly into the simmering water; poach them for 2–3 minutes so the whites are cooked but the yolks still runny. Drain with a slotted spoon on kitchen paper.

5. Pour the vinaigrette over the salad and toss to combine. Divide between four plates and top each with a poached egg. Scatter with the chives and serve.

KCALS	FAT	SAT FAT	CARBS	SUGARS	FIBRE	PROTEIN	SALT
457	35.0g	8.0g	15.0g	1.0g	2.0g	19.0g	1.99g

Crispy Fennel Pork Chops

with Pan-fried Fennel

Serves:
2

Equipment:
Frying pan

Cook's Notes:
The addition of a little touch of Chinese five spice gives this classic combination a hint of the Orient.

2 tbsp olive oil

bunch of spring onions, cut into 2cm (¾in) pieces

1 fennel bulb, cut into thin wedges

1 tsp fennel seeds

good pinch of Chinese five spice

2 thin boneless pork chops

1 tsp white wine vinegar

1. Heat half the oil in a frying pan and fry the spring onions and fennel for 5–6 minutes over a medium–high heat until they begin to soften and become golden. Add the spices and cook for a minute more, tossing the onions and fennel until coated, then remove from the pan and set aside.

2. Season the pork chops with salt and pepper. Increase the heat and fry the chops for 2–3 minutes on each side until lovely and golden and nearly cooked through.

3. Return the spring onions and fennel to the pan with a splash of water and the vinegar. Bubble for 1 minute, then serve.

KCALS	FAT	SAT FAT	CARBS	SUGARS	FIBRE	PROTEIN	SALT
549	41.0g	11.0g	8.0g	4.0g	4.0g	35.0g	0.37g

Spicy Lamb Meatballs

with Chickpea Salad

Serves:
4

Equipment:
Large frying pan,
small saucepan

Cook's Notes:
If you want to get this on the table even faster, you can buy great ready-made lamb meatballs in most supermarkets. Just add the garlic and spices as you fry them up.

2 tsp cumin seeds

450g (1lb) lamb mince

4 garlic cloves, crushed

good pinch of chilli flakes

2 tbsp olive oil

1 x 400g (14oz) tin chickpeas

2 tbsp extra-virgin olive oil

200g (7oz) low-fat
natural yoghurt

1 tbsp rose harissa paste

150g (5oz) rocket
or baby lettuce leaves

large handful of flat-leaf
parsley, leaves picked

large handful of coriander,
leaves picked

1. Toast the cumin seeds in a dry frying pan over a medium heat until aromatic, then remove and set aside.

2. Put the lamb mince in a bowl with half the toasted cumin seeds, half the garlic and the chilli flakes. Season well with salt and pepper and shape into 12–14 meatballs.

3. Heat the olive oil in a large frying pan and brown the meatballs really well all over, then add a splash of water and cook for 2–3 minutes more until the meatballs are cooked through.

4. Drain and rinse the chickpeas and tip into a bowl. Add the extra-virgin olive oil and remaining cumin seeds and garlic. Mix the yoghurt and harissa paste together in a separate bowl.

5. Toss the chickpeas with the leaves and herbs, then serve with the meatballs and the harissa yoghurt on the side.

KCALS	FAT	SAT FAT	CARBS	SUGARS	FIBRE	PROTEIN	SALT
458	30.0g	9.0g	14.0g	4.0g	5.0g	30.0g	0.48g

Index

Metric/Imperial Conversion Chart

All equivalents are rounded, for practical convenience.

Weight

25g	1 oz
50g	2 oz
100g	3½ oz
150g	5 oz
200g	7 oz
250g	9 oz
300g	10 oz
400g	14 oz
500g	1 lb 2 oz
1 kg	2¼ lb

Length

1cm	½ inch
2.5cm	1 inch
20cm	8 inches
25cm	10 inches
30cm	12 inches

Oven Temperatures

Celsius	Fahrenheit
140	275
150	300
160	325
180	350
190	375
200	400
220	425
230	450

Volume

5ml		1 tsp
15ml		1 tbsp
30ml	1 fl oz	2 tbsp
60ml	2 fl oz	4 tbsp
75ml		⅓ cup
100ml	3 ½ fl oz	
125ml	4 fl oz	½ cup
150ml	5 fl oz	¾ cup
175ml	6 fl oz	¾ cup
250ml	8 fl oz	1 cup
1 litre	1 quart	4 cups

Volume *(dry ingredients – an approximate guide)*

butter	1 cup (2 sticks) = 225g
rolled oats	1 cup = 100g
fine powders (e.g. flour)	1 cup = 125g
breadcrumbs (fresh)	1 cup = 50g
breadcrumbs (dried)	1 cup = 125g
nuts (e.g. almonds)	1 cup = 125g
seeds (e.g. chia)	1 cup = 160g
dried fruit (e.g. raisins)	1 cup = 150g
dried legumes (large, e.g. chickpeas)	1 cup = 170g
grains, granular goods and small dried legumes (e.g. rice, quinoa, sugar, lentils)	1 cup = 200g
grated cheese	1 cup = 100g

Thank You!

To my endlessly supportive and highly patient Sofie, who takes care of us all and brings the calm to my madness. Love you, lovely lady!

Our little Noah, for sampling the goods and being such an adventurous eater – you've changed the way we cook at home for the better!

To my brilliant food editor Lizzie Kamenetzky, for your brilliant no-nonsense approach to eating well and for all the work put in to make this book what it is.

My fearless leaders at United Agents: Rosemary Scoular and Aoife Rice. Rosemary for cracking the whip and giddying me up into gear to get things done – thank you for seeing this book through from start to finish.

Our brilliant little team at Hodder in the UK: Tamsin English, Nicky Ross, Natalie Bradley, Caitriona Horne and Steven Cooper.

Thank you Nathan Burton for the cover and interior design of the book and for patiently putting up with my changes.

To Issy Croker and Emily Ezekiel for making the food look so beautiful throughout this book.

To Clare Sayer for crossing the 't's, dotting the 'i's and generally making sense of my text – always a pleasure to work together. Kerry Torrens for providing all our recipes with nutritional breakdowns.

To my cousin and make-up artist to the stars, Susan Yates, for scrubbing me up well for the cover!

My assistant Adam Kaufmann, for always making life that little bit easier!

To Brian Walsh at RTE, a massive thank you for steering each TV project we work on so seamlessly.

To Suzanne Weldon and Helen Sommerville and all of the SPAR crew who have supported me from day one.

To our brilliant team at our production company, Appetite Media. Robin Murray, Marc Dillon, Faye McCarthy, Paul Kehoe, Mark Boland, Karen Convery, Chloe Chan and Sarah Watchorn for bringing the recipes in this book to life so beautifully in the accompanying TV series.

Finally, thank you to my family and friends, who are regular guinea pigs for all the recipes!